George W. Gilmore

Korea of today

George W. Gilmore

Korea of today

ISBN/EAN: 9783743345539

Manufactured in Europe, USA, Canada, Australia, Japa

Cover: Foto ©ninafisch / pixelio.de

Manufactured and distributed by brebook publishing software (www.brebook.com)

George W. Gilmore

Korea of today

BUDDHIST MONKS

T. NELSON AND SONS

London, Edinburgh, and New York

1894

CONTENTS.

I.	THE COUNTRY,	7
II.	THE GOVERNMENT,	17
III.	THE CAPITAL,	26
IV.	THE LANGUAGES,	36
V.	THE PEOPLE,	44
VI.	MANNERS AND CUSTOMS,	54
VII.	MANNERS AND CUSTOMS.—(*Continued*),	64
VIII.	FASHIONS,	72
IX.	PLEASURES AND SOLEMNITIES,	78
X.	RELIGIONS AND SUPERSTITIONS,	89
XI.	RESOURCES,	99
XII.	PROGRESS,	111
XIII.	FOREIGN RELATIONS,	117
XIV.	MISSIONS,	125

Much of this book has been extracted from "Corea from its Capital," by G. W. Gilmore, M.A. New matter has been added with special reference to the present crisis.

COREA OF TO-DAY.

CHAPTER I.

THE COUNTRY.

WHEN the writer first announced to a college friend his intention of going to Corea, that friend replied, "I have a vague recollection that there is such a place somewhere on the eastern coast of Asia, but I must get down my atlas and definitely settle its position in my mind." Geographical knowledge is often very vague. People have very often only a "general idea" of a place, and so a word or two on the geographical position of Corea may not be amiss.

The most direct way of going to the country—a description of which will settle its geographical position—is by crossing America to San Francisco or Vancouver. Taking ship at Vancouver, we sail almost directly west, and so run into the harbour of Yokohama, Japan. Now, if the steamer could push on through the Japanese Islands, we should run into a peninsula jutting out from the east coast of Asia toward the south-east. This peninsula is the country of which we are speaking. Looked at from Canada, it is directly behind Japan.

This little country of Corea, or, as the natives call it, Cho Son, the "Land of Morning Calm," whose king is "monarch of ten thousand isles," has been the last to open its gates for the entrance of foreigners within its boundaries. The persistent exclusion of all foreigners from its territory has gone so far that mariners shipwrecked on its shores have been detained as prisoners, in order that no news might through them reach other nations to tempt incursions for booty or conquest. But practically the whole world is now open to Western civilization. There is not a single independent country from which foreigners are excluded. Tibet, it is true, still frets at the visits of curious tourists, but that little corner is only a province of China.

It was the expectation of many that, when Corea was opened up to the world, its people would be found savage, uncouth, and forbidding in their manners. What must have been their surprise, therefore, to find that not only were the people of Corea not of this description, but that, on the contrary, in no countries in the East, Japan and India not excepted, were foreigners so cordially welcomed, so kindly received, and so right royally treated! As a visitor passes along the crowded streets of the capital, he has not to elbow his way through by main force or by turning himself "edgewise," as in the thoroughfares of our own cities, and he is surprised to find that nearly all Coreans, when they see a foreigner coming, turn aside and give the right of way to the new-comer. And this comes not through fear nor through contempt; the movement is one of native courtesy: the Coreans consider foreigners the *guests* of the country, and as such to be treated with all respect. Similarly, when the king takes an outing in state, crowds flock to see the sight, and line the streets six or eight deep. At such times, if the cry goes up, "Here comes a foreigner!" a passage is opened for the lucky man, and he can walk through the crowd and take a front place without the slightest murmur from any one.

The question, therefore, naturally arises, If this is the disposition of the inhabitants, if they are so universally courteous and hospitable, how shall we explain the policy of isolation which was adhered to till within eight years—a policy which refused to the Chinese, who claimed suzerainty over Corea, the right to a resident, and even compelled an ambassador from the Emperor of China, on the rare occasions when one made a visit, to enter the country with only the scantiest train of attendants? The answer to this, as to many other questions, lies in the position of the peninsula between China and Japan.

The history of Corea is a peculiarly chequered one. Were we to trace it, the one fact which would stand out before us is the frequent invasions from China on the north and Japan on the south. While the Chinese have time and again attempted to subjugate the peninsula, occasionally for a time adding it as a province to China, the Japanese have held from the second century of our era that Corea is a part of Japan. The consequence has been that hordes, sometimes reckoned at a million of men, have been sent like tidal-waves from China, carrying devastation in their wake. And again from the south the sturdy and brave soldiers of Japan (and there are no better fighters in the world to-day than the Japanese) have overrun the peninsula toward the north. And not only this: we find the Chinese and the Japanese, whose hate for each other has ever been deadly, fighting out their battles on Corean soil. To this there must be added the incursions of pirates from the Japan coast and islands, who have ravaged the coasts of Corea, burned the cities, and kept the inhabitants of the peninsula in a state of constant fear. It is no wonder then that the Coreans have reasoned thus: "If our own cousins, those of Mongolian origin, the people of straight black hair, oblique eyes, and yellow skin, treat us in this fashion; if they know no use for us but to burn our cities, plunder our territory, and kill and capture our people, what must we expect from barbarians of the West? We'll none of them." And so, isolated from all that she could keep out, rejecting all overtures, preventing, as far as

COREA AND JAPAN. 11

possible, all news concerning herself from reaching the outside world, the hermit nation has lived in content, shut in and confined to her own resources, until the last decades of the nineteenth century only have seen treaties made with Western powers.

Of course, we are not to forget that a start was made in the direction of opening up the ports of Corea when, in 1876, a treaty was made with the Japanese by which Japan once for all gave up her claims to the peninsula, and acknowledged the independence of the sister country. Its chief significance, however, was in its opening a port of Corea to trade with the Japanese. The hermit condition was by this act abandoned. The way was paved for other nations to ask the same with some reasonable ground of expectation that it would be granted. A treaty with the United States was negotiated in 1882. Others soon followed with England, Russia, Italy, and France, and the hermit nation is a hermit no longer.

The peninsula presents to the casual tourist none of the attractions of Japan. The traveller will find here no interesting temples set in groves of beautiful cryptomeria. There are no picturesque shrines in lovely valleys, few wooded hills inviting the traveller to rest, no art-producing workshops, a delight to the eyes, and suggesting a depletion of the purse. The country in the neighbourhood of the capital is denuded of forests. The hills, bereft of their mantle of tree and bush, lie open to the baking sun and the wearing rain, their gaunt sides furrowed and seamed with channels worn by the midsummer floods.

The sail up the coast brings to view no beauties of cultivation such as are seen in passing through the Inland Sea of Japan. Only bleak hills, rugged crags, here and there in a recess the few low huts of a fishing village, clustered together on a lonely shore washed by surging tides of nearly thirty feet, which, sweeping out, leave bare vast mud-flats and dreary weed-covered rocks. Its shores are rocky and hemmed in by dangerous shoals and treacherous rocks.

Only a vivid imagination could regard Corea as a land worthy of the visit of people who seek wealth either by robbery or by industry. One going there must be prepared to see a country with apparently no resources. Its people seem slothful and unambitious; its towns and villages appear unhealthy and its homes uninviting. It is only during a longer sojourn than tourists can generally afford that aught attractive really comes to the surface.

In passing through Japan every turn brings into view something to charm the sense. Interesting faces, pretty costumes, neat homes, careful agriculture, grotesque horticulture, sprightliness, wit and grace, all abound there; and with all there is to be seen an inherent politeness in the people that bestows additional charms upon all besides. In the Corean peninsula faces appear dull, costumes repeating each other

grow monotonous, houses are poor and without adornment, agriculture is neglected, and landscape gardening is unknown, excepting crude attempts at the graves of the nobility, while the people look dull and uninteresting, gazing with open mouth at any unusual sight, and seeming at times bereft even of mother wit. Corea is decidedly not a country for tourists.

In its physical features, Corea much resembles Japan. It is very mountainous, though the mountains nowhere reach a great height. The backbone of the peninsula runs near the north-eastern coast. From this, spurs run out towards the sea.

The climate of the capital, which is in the latitude of Lisbon, is delightful, except for about six weeks in midsummer. Sudden alternations of heat and cold are unknown there. Snow often lies on the ground from the middle of December to the middle of February, but at no time does the cold become unbearable. I have never seen the thermometer below zero, though for nearly a month the mercury in a sheltered place did not vary 15°, running from about 5' to 20°. Thus there is in midwinter a level of cold. About February 1, the mercury begins to rise, until by March 15 people are making gardens. The temperature continues to rise till about July 15, when the summer level of about 90° is reached, with, however, but few nights when the heat makes sleeping difficult. This is the rainy season. And how it rains! Apparently the water falls in sheets. Clouds roll across and drop their loads, and then roll back and double their contribution. Not steadily, but often with a day or two of fine weather succeeding a day or two of successive, almost continuous, showers, until, about September 1, the magnificent autumn weather commences. This is the crown of the year. Delightful days, bright and sunny temperature, almost imperceptibly falling, up to the middle of December. I have played tennis on December 16, and gone skating at Christmas.

Thus there seem no unusual drafts on the resident's strength, and, with the care necessary in the East, life in Corea is healthy and pleasant.

CHAPTER II.

THE GOVERNMENT.

IN this chapter we shall deal with the composition and internal administration of the Corean government. The relations of the country to the neighbouring nations demand a separate chapter.

Power centres in the king, or *hapmun*, or *ingum*, as he is called by the people. The functions of government are all exercised in his name by ministers presumably appointed by him, and acting under his authority. The people have no share in the government, and no authority proceeds from them. In Cho Son truly "le roi c'est l'état." From the king, power filters through a line of officials down to the head man of the smallest village, each official requiring from those beneath him an account of whatever transpires in his own jurisdiction.

Yet, although the people have no voice in the selection of officers, and no direct way of controlling the actions of the government, when measures distasteful to the mass of the inhabitants have been decided on, there is what might be called a popular protest by the mass of citizens, in the shape of a sort of ferment, at first unnoticeable, but increasing in degree until a state of excitement ensues, when business is neglected and mass-meetings are held, until the news reaches the palace that the people are displeased. So far as I could learn—and the phenomena under discussion appeared several times during my residence in Corea—these popular protests, if founded on right, are effective in producing a change in the policy. If, however, the excitement has been caused by false rumours, if mischief-makers have circulated false reports, and, owing to these, misapprehensions are abroad, the usual course is for proclamations to be posted in the great square of the metropolis, correcting the misunderstanding and advising the people to return to their occupations. If, however, this is not effective, as is sometimes the case, a second proclamation is issued, in a different tone. The tenor of the first may be gentle and fatherly; that of the second is sterner, and gives the impression that "business is meant." Generally a day or two is allowed for this to have its effect, when, if the excitement does not subside, the military are put into service, the streets patrolled, disturbers of the peace arrested and punished, and so the trouble is settled. Thus the populace have a way of making their wishes known and their power felt even to the heart of the palace.

The king has as his immediate counsellors and assistants three men, who are called the "prime min-

DEGREES OF "RANK."

ister" and ministers of the "right" and the "left." These three are the chief men in the kingdom, and out-rank all others. After these come the heads of the departments, six in number. These are assisted by numerous officials of different rank all the way down to the pettiest official, who is of the standing of our village constable. The whole matter of "rank" or *pessal* is very intricate. There are in Corea two kinds of rank, civil and military (Corea has no navy). Of these the higher is the civil. Both civil and military rank are divided into a large number of grades of office-holders, separated from one another with the finest discrimination. When a man, by passing an examination, gets "rank," he becomes an office-holder, so that all "men of rank" are office-holders. A man on becoming an office-holder is assigned to some duty, and is thereupon in the line of promotion. He is supposed to get his pickings at the public crib, and the people at large furnish the fodder.

With all these ramifications of rank it ought to be an easy matter to secure responsibility and good government. But, unfortunately, the possession of official position makes it possible to oppress the people with but little danger of punishment. There seems to be a tacit agreement among the nobility to suppress any attempt on the part of the common people to carry information against one official to another. While we were in the country, our cook was becoming quite a wealthy man. He had bought two houses, and had besides a little ready money; but he told me that he wished to continue to work for foreigners. On being asked for the reason, he said that were he not in the employ of foreigners, he would be immediately sought by some of the officials for the purpose of *lending* them thirty or forty thousand cash (about five pounds). As this loan would of course never be returned, it would amount to a levy on his property. So long as he was employed by foreigners he, in accordance with treaty stipulations in such a case, could not be arrested except through their own consulate, and he was consequently safe from the exactions of the petty officials. It became very clear to me that exactions of this sort were exceedingly common in Corea. If it became known that a man had laid up an amount of cash, an official would seek a loan. If it were refused, the man would be thrown into prison on some trumped-up charge. The supposed criminal would be whipped every morning until he had met the demands, or had by his obstinacy scared the officials into apprehensions for their own safety, or until some of his relations had paid the amount demanded, or some compromise had been made.

But this is not the only method of obtaining money. Not only is a person liable for his own debts, but even for those of his relations. The filching officials often take advantage of this, and not being able to arrest the moneyed member of the family, they will arrest a cousin or brother, and then demand payment.

When the unfortunate fellow protests that he has no money, and cannot possibly pay, the officers will coolly retort, "Oh, well, we know that. But your cousin has plenty. Get him to pay your fine." So close are the bonds of family relationship that this method is usually effectual.

When travellers speak of the poverty and indolence of the Coreans, it must not be taken for granted that this is altogether the result of their temperament. It must be remembered that the people have no incentive to labour. Their laziness is not innate, but results from a knowledge that all fruit of toil, above what is required for the veriest necessities, is liable to be stolen from them by corrupt and insatiate officials, against whom they are powerless.

Appeals to the supreme power are exceedingly difficult from the fact, already mentioned, that officials are chary of listening to complaints against one of their number. So it is a very rare occurrence for His Majesty to hear of the wrong-doings of his subordinates. Besides this, there is a custom among them that the king must hear no unpleasant news if it is possible to prevent such reaching him. Of course, when wrong has been done to a man of another nationality, the wrong comes to the king's ear through diplomatic or consular channels, and then punishment is swift and sure.

But not only in the ways indicated above, do officials abuse their power. There is besides a great deal of nepotism in the ranks. It is a fact that the sons of high officials are invariably, before reaching the age of maturity, well advanced in official position.

While examinations are held for the purpose of finding scholars who are capable of taking part in the administration of government, these scholars are most frequently found among the sons of officials. The examiners, having received a bribe, can easily find the paper of the briber, and, by ostentatiously showing it to His Majesty, gain for the writer a high grade.*

A picture of the parade which attends official life is thus given by a recent writer:—

"About the courts of the *yong mun* (official residence) is at all times a great crowd of attendants, police runners and soldiers, in coarse uniforms of variegated colours indicating their position. These pass the orders of the great man within in long-drawn, shrill cries, heard long distances away from the *yong mun;* they come and go, carrying and bringing mes-

---

* My own teacher, an exceptionally honourable as well as well-read man, told me that he would very much like to obtain rank, but said he could not do so, as he had not the money or the influence necessary. Asked how it was that either was necessary when the examination was held to find ability, he said, "Very true; but very many papers are written. The king sees only a few, and those are selected by the assistants of His Majesty. If I knew one of these men, I might persuade him to see my paper and show it, or I might brighten his eyes with some cash." Asking him how much cash would be needed, he said, "Oh, perhaps a hundred thousand" (over ten pounds). I then said, "Suppose I should offer to lend you that amount?" To this his reply was, "You are very kind, and I appreciate your offer, but it is not according to my conscience to get rank in that way."

sages. Squatting with heads close to the ground, they speak in stage tones to the officer in the high place within from morning to night, at both of which times, at the opening and closing of the gates, there is a great noise of drums, of shrill fifes, and of weird cries; all seems bustle and confusion, believed to be necessary to the dignity of the officers. I was lodged in a *kilchung* or guest-house, off the main courtyard. A host of braves was detailed to provide for me. Their attentions were painful in time. If I tried to take a nap, the word went forth, 'The great man sleeps; be still,' and in a little time a continuous wrangle and racket began, preventing all sleep, in the efforts of the braves to keep each other quiet, and the vigorous thrashing of citizens who came to get a peep at the foreigner. Meals appeared six times the first day, seven the second; and at short intervals during the day an officer appeared to ask if I had eaten well, and, if so, to thank me."

In the administration of state affairs there is a strange combination of shrewdness, want of judgment, and indecision which is decidedly Oriental. The opening of the country to trade necessitated the adoption of customs regulations, and the collection of customs was placed under the administration of the Chinese service, then under the direction of Sir Henry Parkes. This was probably the best arrangement that could have been made, for it has insured a faithful and careful handling of the customs. At the present time the customs service of Corea is really a part of the customs service of China, though no part of the duties collected goes into the Chinese treasury. All surplus remaining over the cost of administering the service goes into the Corean treasury. The government is deriving a considerable and steadily increasing sum from this source.

The other government departments are under native officials, who seem fated to fail in all the enterprises which they undertake. Thus, the government derives some revenue from the raising of silk, and so an expert was engaged to look after the cultivation of the silk-worm. This became a burden on the government's hands; for after an engagement of about five years, the expert left his position, the only result of his years' service to the government being some small mulberry orchards of sickly growth, and probably not a pound has come, or will come, to repay the hundreds expended in his services and in the planting of the orchard. Similar failures, as we shall see, have attended the attempts to establish a mint, to open coal mines, and to enlarge and organize the army.

Each of these enterprises, except perhaps that of the army improvement, might have done well and have brought good returns. But they all stopped short of thoroughness, of actual use.

Perhaps the root of the whole matter lies here: the king has had a "foreign adviser," a gentleman who

JEALOUSY TOWARDS FOREIGNERS.

has advised *against* these various enterprises. But the jealousy toward foreigners, which hampers all such as engage with the Corean government, made the employment of this gentleman a farce, the money paid to him a sheer waste, and the enterprises of the government pure loss.

The question now is, whether in time the king and his advisers will let common sense in these matters guide them, and whether they will not intrust to those foreigners whom they engage full control of the matters they are appointed to manage. If they are content to let competent men direct such matters, the finances of the kingdom and the government itself can soon be put in excellent condition.

CHAPTER III.

THE CAPITAL.

WE are accustomed to speak of the capital of Corea as "Seoul," supposing that to be the name of the town. Really that word means "the capital," and the name of the capital is Kyung-gi-do or Kyung-gi.

The first impression one receives on passing a night there is that somehow one has gone back to the middle ages. It has a decidedly medieval flavour to find oneself in a walled town with the gates shut, going about after dark, with lantern in hand, in streets otherwise unlighted and quite deserted by men, with no possibility of exit except by scaling the walls.

The capital of Corea, occupying in that peninsula a position much like that of Rome in Italy, about twenty-eight miles from its port, called Chemulpo, is a town estimated to contain 250,000 to 400,000 inhabitants, including those villages clustered on the outside beneath the walls. The city proper is enclosed by a wall from twenty to thirty feet in height, crowned with battlements and pierced with embra-

THE CITY WALL.

sures, not, however, for cannon, but for bowmen. Behind the wall is a mound of earth which forms a vantage-ground for the defenders in case of attack. The excellence of the construction of this wall will be understood when it is known that it has been built about five hundred years, and is now in excellent repair except in a few places. It has not, however, a smooth surface, but can be scaled at very many points, and at intervals there are found well-worn traces where late arrivals enter or leave the city between the times of closing and opening the gates.

The wall is pierced by eight gates, one of which is secret, leading by a hidden path to the fortress of Pook Hon, and is for the purpose of affording the king an escape in times of danger. The road can be very speedily destroyed behind him, so as to make pursuit impossible. These gates are set in arches about sixteen feet deep, made of large blocks of stone finely hewn and joined, which furnish as perfect specimens of arch-building as can be seen in any country. The gates themselves are but sorry affairs in comparison with the strong wall and the magnificent arches. They are surmounted by typical structures of wood, one or two stories in height, which make the gates very picturesque objects and the sure cynosure of the tourist's lens.

The great wall scales two hills in its circuit round the city. About the centre, on the south, is a bold, well-wooded, and beautiful hill about eight hundred feet in height, rising abruptly from its base, and showing in some places sheer precipices of a hundred feet. This is called Nam San, or South Mountain. Diagonally across the city, toward the north-west, is another hill, higher and with a less dense covering of trees, in many places only large bare crags appearing. This is called Pook San, or North Mountain.

Inside the walls, the impression of medievalism is by no means removed. The visitor finds only three wide streets in Seoul. One of these almost traverses the city from east to west, ending at the great east gate. The others run off at right angles from this, one of them to the main gates of the palace, and the other to the great south gate. Only one of these is kept clear so that its entire width can be seen at all times—namely, the one leading to the palace. In the others, booths and shops are built, so that only a narrow way wide enough for ox-carts is left.

All the other streets are narrow and winding, and in many of them it is barely possible for men on foot to squeeze past each other. A close investigation, however, shows that, as originally laid out, the streets were not so contracted. Gradually the owners on each side have encroached on the road, until they have almost closed up the public way. Through these streets, owing to their narrowness and to the projecting thatch and tiling of the roofs, a single mounted man often finds it difficult to ride, and must pass carefully along, bowing his head and

OUTSIDE WALL SHOWING STREET AND VEILED WOMEN.

Page 27.

PALACE ENCLOSURES.

swaying in his saddle, to avoid being swept from his seat.

There are now three palace enclosures in the city. That occupied at present by the royal family is immediately under the North Mountain. Another enclosure was formerly occupied by a regent, afterwards used as a mint, and is now fallen into a woful state of dilapidation. The grounds are occupied by mulberry groves planted by the government for the fostering of the silk industry. The third, which was until a very few years ago the residence of the royal family, is a large enclosure containing very many pretty buildings now fast falling into decay, and is of such great extent that there is said to be the lair of a tigress and her cubs in the thickets near the back. There has been some attempt at landscape gardening; but, unfortunately, it is a persistent notion of the Coreans that the grounds about a residence should be cut up by walls, each set of buildings being enclosed and thus shut off entirely from the rest.

The houses of the Coreans may be divided into two classes according to the materials of their roofs —thatch or tile. The poorer ones are of course thatched. The typical shape of a peasant's hut is that of a horse-shoe, with one side resting on the street, and the court in the centre. The houses are separated one from another by high walls, so that a view of a neighbour's yard is impracticable. The houses are of one story, only a few buildings used for shops having two. The Coreans do not seem to care for gardening, nor have I ever seen a house with lawns laid out about it. Some cultivate a few flowers, especially chrysanthemums and hollyhocks. The houses of the more wealthy are distinguished by occupying more ground, by being built in a square around a hollow court, and by having tiled roofs. Besides this, the grounds are entered through large gates, and contain not only the residence of the owner, but sometimes a great number of small out-buildings, which are the homes of the retainers and servants, besides wood-houses and store-houses of various descriptions. The ground is by no means all built up, and there is unoccupied space enough inside the walls to furnish a large portion of the population with food should the city be besieged.

It speaks volumes for the orderly character of the people that one sees no police in the daytime. Police duty is done at night by the soldiers, and private watchmen are also engaged, at least by some of the foreigners and by the legations. Very rarely, except in times of popular excitement, is there to be seen anything that suggests the need of a police force. Very rare indeed is the sight of a man in an uproarious state of intoxication. Not more than two such cases came under my observation during a residence of over two years. Not more than a dozen cases of intoxication in any form met my eye, and these were generally of men lying in a stupor and sleeping off the effects of their potations. Occasionally there was a fight, the usual method in such cases being for the belligerents to drag each other about by the hair.

Not the least strange of a newly-arrived foreigner's sensations after nightfall is the perfect stillness of the city. After dark the only sounds are the occasional howl of a dog, or, in summer, the shrill piping of the frogs (frogs piping in a city of two hundred thousand inhabitants!), or the patter of the ironing-sticks as the housewife smooths out the coat of her lord for the morrow's outing. If the stranger feels the stillness oppressive, and leaves his room for a stroll, he will find a lantern a necessity, for the city is not lighted, and as he looks out over the dwellings he will see but few indications of the existence of the thousands of inhabitants. As he passes through the streets he may see a figure dart hastily through a doorway, as though to be abroad were a misdemeanour; or he may meet a solitary woman, or, mayhap, a little company, at least one of them carrying a lantern, passing quietly along, with faces carefully shielded from observation. He may meet the patrol—two soldiers armed with musket or native flint-lock—sauntering in a loose-jointed manner round their beat; but so silent is the city that his own footfalls re-echo unpleasantly from the walls, as though he were in a city of the dead. Here and there a door standing ajar will show a group of men in a small room lighted by a rushlight, playing a game very much like go-bang; or perhaps a company listening while one of them sings a solo, and they all join in the chorus; or they may take turns in telling delightful little stories, of which there is in Corea a great abundance. After going back to his lodging, if he is entertained where a private watchman is engaged, he may just be sinking into a doze when he will be aroused by a sound entirely new to him—that of a staff with strips of metal fastened loosely upon it struck sharply on the ground at measured intervals. He may then learn that the custom is for watchmen to carry such staffs, and by striking them on the ground give warning of their approach. Of course a robber is seldom caught; and it always seemed to me that the one object of this rattle was to keep up the courage of the watchman.

If the visitor wakes early in the morning, and takes a walk through the town, he will find the scene transformed, and as he nears the centre of the city the clangour of the morning market will assail his ears. He will find wooden platforms in the middle of the street, covered with dried fish, fruit, greens, rice, and all the varied articles composing the Corean's diet, and their owners crying out the virtue of their wares in thorough Western fashion; for the people are early risers, and in summer five to six o'clock is high

SIGNAL-FIRES. 35

market-time. By eight o'clock, or very little later, the streets are pretty well cleared of these articles of a perishable nature, and then purchases must be made at the shops or booths.

The impression of medievalism will be heightened, if the foreigner is, about sunset, in a position whence he can see the summit of Nam San and the other peaks about the city. He will see first one fire, then another, and another, until at least four fires are burning. These are the terminals of as many series of fires, signalling from the remote provinces that all is well and the kingdom at peace. Immediately the palace bell is rung, and officials go to the palace to report to His Majesty the doings of the day in the several departments of public business. About the same time one near the west gate will find his ears assailed by sounds which are new, unless he has visited China. These will be found to proceed from a Corean band at the residence of the governor, just outside the wall, whose duty it is to play an evening serenade. The gates of the city are closed soon after nightfall, at about half-past eight or nine o'clock, no exact time being set. About nine o'clock the strokes of a huge bell near the centre of the town may be heard resounding through the city, deeply and richly resonant if struck in time, and this signal corresponds to the curfew in Norman England, sounding the hour for people to retire from the streets.

CHAPTER IV.

THE LANGUAGES.

COREA is bilingual. Not that two languages are spoken, but two are used. Thus we find a spoken and a written language, differing in vocabulary, in grammar, and in writing, in existence side by side.

The vernacular is a native language exactly like the Japanese in grammar, but differing from it in vocabulary, excepting only in the case of those words which have been borrowed from the Chinese, or have been derived from a common ancestry. This is the language spoken by everybody, from the king down. The great difficulty a foreigner finds in acquiring it arises from its euphonic changes and its "honorifics." One who has not had much drill in languages finds the euphony very perplexing, as the roots of verbs are often so modified by the influence of endings and by contraction as to be almost unrecognizable. The "honorifics" are also most perplexing, and yet a thorough mastery of them is essential. The endings of words must be carefully altered according to the grade of the person addressed. There is a different ending for almost every grade. As a rule, it may be said that the longer the ending attached to the verb, the greater the respect for the person addressed. A new-comer who has not mastered these difficult points, is very apt to confuse his endings; and it has happened that when a host wished courteously to invite a Corean visitor to dismount and enter and rest, the mistake has been made of peremptorily *ordering* him to get down and go into the house. On the contrary, a lady has been known to use to her servant the politest forms of language; such, for instance, as would be equivalent to asking him to "have the extreme condescension to go and bring in a scuttle of coal."

Even the greetings are graded for different ranks. The three most in use are, "Are you well?" used to inferiors; "Have you been free from sickness?" or, "May you be free from sickness!" more honorific than the preceding; and "May you have peace!" which is the most complimentary.

Coreans realize the difficulties of their language for foreigners, and make great allowances for the mistakes which they make in using it. The belief of the people that others cannot learn their language often puts the Coreans into rather ludicrous positions. More than once, when passing through a part of the capital not much frequented by foreigners, we have seen articles we desired to purchase. On stopping and inquiring the price, we have been amused by the assumption of the shopkeeper that we could not understand his answer, and have watched his most extraordinary pantomimic exertions as he tried to show the value of the things, counting on his fingers, or laying out coins to show the price, notwithstanding that he had been addressed in Corean, and had grasped the meaning. After looking mystified for a while, we would suddenly ask the man if he spoke Corean, at which he would look astonished and say, "Yeh, yeh" (yes, yes), and we would tell him to do so; at which the bystanders, who are generally quick at a joke, would laugh, and sometimes bore the fellow with their badinage.

Along with the spoken or vernacular, we find the Chinese as the medium of correspondence, of official documents, etc. Almost all works of a philosophical, religious, or ethical character are in Chinese. Those who make any pretensions to scholarship must read Chinese easily and write it correctly. It is that without which no one can hold office. Hence it is probable that at least one-third, perhaps one-half, of the male population is tolerably well versed in both Corean and Chinese, for nearly all males are eligible for office.

Reference has been made to the examinations held for promotion to official position. As these vary only in importance and in the numbers attending them, a description of one will suffice.

These examinations, or *quagas*, are held in the enclosure behind the palace, and to them come candidates from all parts of the country. The examinations are

THE QUAGAS.

not conducted like those in China, where each candidate is shut up in a little compartment until he has produced his thesis. On the contrary, the competition is in an open field, where the candidates work, some in the heat of the sun, some under the shade of a large umbrella, some of the more wealthy under tents. Passing about among the candidates are numbers of vendors of sweets, cakes, and various drinks. Attendants and officials and soldiers swarm in crowds. On one side of the field is a massive stone platform, where His Majesty, who is supposed to be the arbiter of the contest, remains during the examination. Soldiers armed with muskets and various firearms, native and foreign, antique and modern, march or lounge around: side by side may be seen two soldiers, one armed with a repeating rifle of excellent make, with sabre-bayonet fixed, and the other bearing a native flint-lock, fired not when pressed against the shoulder, but held out at arm's length. These guards do not seem to be there for the purpose of watching the candidates, or to prevent unfair advantages being taken. Their sole purpose seems to be to add to the pomp of the occasion. The candidates are all known by their tall horse-hair caps, which distinguish them as far as they can be seen. They range in age from boys to hoary-headed veterans, from the silken and fur-robed noble to the cotton-clad peasant. When their papers are finished, they are signed, rolled up neatly, and then thrown at the foot of the royal platform.

We once saw a boy come up gaily, with a bright and happy face, and, with a careless laugh, gleefully pitch down his paper, evidently casting hardly a thought upon this his first essay in literature. Thence his paper was picked up and carried to be placed on the platform, where it would be lost in the pile which soon became many feet in length. Soon after we saw approach an old man, who pushed his way through the throng, and then, with anxiety written on every line in his face, carefully poising his paper in the air, he threw it at the feet of a servant, who picked it up without a thought that in that paper were concentrated the study of a lifetime, and perhaps the last hopes of an old man of gaining that goal of a Corean's desires, official position. We saw the old man stoop and crane his neck as he saw his last venture carried up and laid away in the pile, with nothing to distinguish it from the hundreds which lay there; and then, as he saw it safely laid away, with a sigh that reached our hearts and aroused our sympathy, he turned away, hoping against hope, and gathering up his writing-tablet and his equipments, he slowly wended his way home.

The severity of these examinations is undoubtedly very great. They are often on some important subject treated in the Chinese classics. Such questions are asked as, "What does the yih king say is the duty of children at the death of a father?" The answer to such a question necessitates a perfect recollection of a long passage, every character of which must be reproduced with the utmost faithfulness.

Not the least peculiar of the abuses attending these *quagas* is the passing of them by proxy. Thus, a man who finds himself unable from any cause to attend may go to one of his friends and engage him to write a paper for him, paying down a certain amount, from a few shillings to several pounds, and agreeing to pay a much larger sum provided the paper shall secure the prize. One man sometimes passes in no less than four or five papers in a single examination.

The Coreans have many tales connected with the *quaga*, and some of the best of them cluster about a monarch who was the Corean Haroun Al Raschid. One of these runs somewhat as follows:—The king, who loved to go about incognito, that he might find out the condition of his people, one night applied his eye to a crack in a window, and was amazed to find, in a room which betrayed the poverty of the occupants, an old man weeping, a woman singing, and a younger man gaily dancing to the woman's merry notes. The combination was an unusual one, and it aroused the curiosity of the king. He therefore knocked at the entrance, and after a little conversation, in which he played the *rôle* of the belated traveller, he confessed what his curiosity had led him to do, and, mentioning the sight he had beheld, asked an explanation of the peculiar actions. His host, who was the dancer, told the disguised king that he was the son of the old man who wept. The old man, he said, had formerly been wealthy, but through the avarice and oppression of officials had been stripped of his possessions. He had grown very melancholy, and so at eventide the son and his wife were wont to sing and dance, so as to draw the old man's mind from his troubles. The king, not disclosing his identity, then entered into conversation upon topics of national interest, and discovered in his host a man of extraordinary knowledge and discretion, which, coupled with the filial love so admirably shown in the endeavour to cheer his father, quite won the king's heart. He then asked the host whether he proposed to enter the *quaga* taking place on the morrow. To this the reply was given that he had not even heard there was to be one. "Oh yes," said the king; "and if I were you, I would enter. If you take the prize, it will place you above want, and make your father's last days comfortable and bright." The host promised that if there was an examination, he would certainly attend. The king, apologizing for his intrusion, withdrew, and on returning to his palace ordered a proclamation to be posted, giving notice of a *quaga* to be held on the following day. The people of the capital were surprised, for no examination was expected then; but the news flew, and the candidates flocked in. When the subject was given out it was: "A weeping elder, a singing woman, and a dancing man." The candidates, excepting one, were all astonished, and agreed that no such subject was treated in the classics, and wondered how they should proceed. The man who had entertained the king was also lost in wonder, not at how he should treat the subject, but at the coincidence between the subject and his own daily practice. However, he was at home with the theme, and treated it in a skilful and ingenious manner. Upon examination his paper, of course, was the only one which treated the subject adequately, and so he was adjudged the prize. Orders came to him to be present the following day at the court, as he was now an official. He was therefore presented at court, and was astonished to find on the throne his late inquisitive visitor. The king received him kindly, appointed him to a lucrative office, and gained for himself a stanch adherent and an able officer.

CHAPTER V.

THE PEOPLE.

TOURISTS have talked and newspaper correspondents have written as though Coreans were much above the average of mankind in height. There are two possible explanations of this. Those who have either visited or lived in Japan have become accustomed to the diminutive stature of these people, and when among the taller people of Cho Son have naturally magnified the stature of the latter. Another reason for this mistake is found in the garb of the Coreans. It is a well-known fact that a long overcoat adds apparently to a person's height. Now, the Coreans all wear flowing coats, and when we remember that these coats are often white, we can understand the misapprehension of visitors in speaking of their stature. My own observation would lead me to say that the men average a little over five feet six inches in height—perhaps five feet seven.

Their hair is long, straight, black, and coarse. There is a tendency to a dirty, tawny tinge; but as

PHYSIQUE.   45

the hair is an important feature in the toilet of both sexes, this tendency is carefully kept out of sight under oil and a blacking mixture lavishly laid on.

The Coreans in many points of physique seem, as in their geographical position, midway between the Chinese and Japanese. They are on the average much taller than the latter, but probably do not reach the average stature of the former. In colour they are not so dark as the Japanese, nor yet have they the dingy yellow cast of the Chinese. Occasionally one sees a native from the country, whose skin is a dirty brown. Some of them are quite fair, and whiteness of complexion is so valued that the women frequently make use of powder, which they find ready to their hand in the shape of rice flour.

The Corean has the oblique eye, which marks his Mongolian origin. The high cheek-bone is also there, and a decided tendency to the flat nose.

In build the Coreans are generally sturdy, and the impression one gets is that they are a well-developed, strong people. But observers are often surprised to find that they do not have the strength their appearance seems to suggest. Many a time, until we got used to them, we have become impatient at the struggles of servants in raising some article of furniture, and one of us has lifted without unusual exertion what two of them seemed to find a heavy burden. This weakness is doubtless real, not assumed. Their diet is largely rice, and often in times of scarcity not so good as that; lentils and millet, and even barley, furnish them sustenance, while in summer-time many a meal is made on cucumbers!

Corean women live in such seclusion that one sees very few of them. Those whom we have seen are very much shorter than the men, not exceeding the Japanese in stature, averaging not over five feet two inches. They are of heavier mould than their eastern neighbours, having very solid, stout frames, seemingly able to endure any amount of labour.

There is nearly always present a pleasing vivacity, a merry sparkle, in the eye of a Japanese woman. Life for her seems a game or a picnic. But from the Corean woman this sprightliness and vivacity and sparkle are absent. Life for her is a serious and earnest business. But this is not the case with the men. Nowhere can be found a readier appreciation of a joke than in Corea. I remember what laughter there was over a trap we laid for a dishonest attendant.

One of our men had been detected stealing wood. A particularly fine stick had captivated his eye, and he had hidden it under the house, with the intention of taking it home after dark. The place of hiding was discovered, and at dusk a small string was tied to it and attached to a mat in the dining-room, in such a way that the mat would curl up as soon as any one attempted to remove the wood. We waited patiently in the dining-room, playing dominoes, until suddenly

PEASANTS' HUTS.

Page 31.

the mat began to curl, when we rushed out and surrounded the hole by which the man had crept under the house. We then called him out, and summoned the other attendants, among whom were three soldiers. One of these handcuffed the fellow, and awaited orders. A search was then instituted by the servants to discover how we knew what was going on, and we found two or three so overcome with laughter at what they considered the fun of the trap, that they were literally rolling on the floor. For weeks we heard of this story being told by our servants to their visitors, and the table-boy could hardly cross the threshold where the mat lay without a glance at the crack and a smile or chuckle at the stratagem.

Among the people at large there seems to be not the slightest antipathy to foreigners as such. We hear in the Corean peninsula no such names as are applied to men of other climes by the Chinese. The name "foreign devil" never once met my ears, nor in all my intercourse with natives did I hear a word in any way derogatory to foreigners because of their foreign birth. The mass of the people look up to Western people as being of superior powers. Tales of the achievements of our fleets, armies, and guns, which do not in any way equal the actual performances, cause open mouths and staring eyes in the listeners. Left to themselves, the people, rulers and all, would welcome gradual and sensible approaches to the ways of the Western world. There are among the higher officials two parties, conservatives and liberals, the former opposed to, the latter favouring a tendency in the direction that Japan has taken. Among the former the Chinese work, and so they manage to retard Corea's advance.

The masses in the country are exceedingly credulous and excitable. They have most curious notions about the ways and doings of foreigners. As a consequence, reports concerning them, no matter how absurd they may be, find a ready lodgment in the ears of the people. The Chinese ambassador, or "resident," as he calls himself, endeavours by all arts and devices to check the tendency towards opening up the country. For instance, in the summer of 1888, it was found that some boys had been stolen and sold into slavery. This is an act not often accomplished, but it is done sometimes. There was great excitement, and the Chinaman spoken of above fanned the spark into a flame by subtly spreading the report, first, that the Japanese had bought the children and eaten them, then that the foreigners had bought them to make medicine, and then that the eyes of the victims were used in making photographs. As the pages of this book testify, the author was a dabbler in photography, and this report was brought to his ears. The capital was in a ferment of excitement; the populace scowled from beneath lowering eyebrows whenever foreigners were seen in the town. Natives were mobbed, and in two or three cases stamped to death by a crowd, when some mischief-maker cried out, "There goes a child-stealer!" In one case a man leading his own child down the main street was attacked because of such a cry, and only escaped by appealing to a petty official who chanced to be at hand, and by being taken before the chief justice of the city. The passion raged so violently that the king issued a proclamation saying that the reports were false, and commanded quiet. Even this had no effect, and in the course of a day or two it was followed by a stern edict that any one caught circulating such reports would be immediately arrested and punished, and that all disorder would be immediately repressed. In less than ten days the excitement subsided, and where a few days before angry crowds had congregated there were to be seen only the usual number of laughing, happy-go-lucky loungers, merchants, and purchasers. The foreigners had little reason for fear, for very few Coreans possess fire-arms. These are contraband articles, and by treaty stipulation they are not allowed to be sold to the natives.

The people have a wholesome fear of an armed foreigner; hence it would be no feat at all in times of excitement for one well-armed and resolute man to keep a whole street clear and put to flight a large band of evil-disposed persons.

Another trait which is peculiarly Corean is curiosity. In that peninsula this trait is by no means exclusively feminine. It is a question whether the men are not more infected with it than the women. Of course, foreigners are as yet a curiosity; especially is this true of the ladies. Consequently, when foreigners, especially if ladies are in the company, go for a stroll with sight-seeing or shopping as a purpose, they are often followed by a crowd varying from a half-dozen to more than a score of persons, all good-natured, though they often crowd a little too closely for comfort. Every motion is watched, commented upon, and each attempt to speak the language is greeted with a smile of approval and appreciation.

Another characteristic of Coreans is a love of country. They yield not even to the Swiss in their intense patriotism. This was strikingly brought out in a case which came under our immediate observation. When we arrived in Japan, in 1886, Kim Ok Kiun, the man who was at the head of the government at the time of the *emeute* in 1884, and who was charged with directing it, was staying in Yokohama. Staying at the hotel with us was another Corean, who was seldom seen and who hardly ever left his room. We were surprised soon to find that the hotel was guarded, and the Japanese police officers were so stationed that no one could leave the house without being seen. Subsequently we learned that this Corean had come over with the intention of assassinating Kim Ok Kiun, and the suspicion was that he was commissioned by the government, of course secretly, to accomplish that design. At any rate, the Japanese government apprehended him, and sent him back to Corea under guard, delivering him to the officials of his own government. Of course, every one who knew the methods of Oriental governments of the Corean type suspected that he was going to his death, and doubtless so did he. The fact that he had compromised his government would certainly produce that result. Notwithstanding that, as soon as we came in sight of Corean shores, he manifested his delight in ways beyond mistaking; and when we dropped anchor in Chemulpo harbour he came to us, and, pointing to the town, said in English (the only words he knew in that language, and which he had learned from his Japanese guards), "My country. I very glad." We never heard of him after that.

At another time, when some tumblers and tricksters exhibited themselves at our compound, they were asked whether, if Mr. Barnum would engage them "for much money," they would go to America for a year. The reply was, "Very many, many thanks. But they could not," they continued, "leave their country, for they would die of home-sickness."

The vice of the Chinese, opium eating and smoking, is extremely rare. The properties of the drug are known. A Corean once remarked to me that "it is very nice, but it costs too much money for us to buy it." There is no likelihood of its becoming common among the people.

CHAPTER VI.

MANNERS AND CUSTOMS.

IT is in the social life of the Coreans that we find the greatest contrast with our own institutions. The key to Corean life lies in the seclusion of the women. As one passes through the streets or along the roads one sees very few females. Most of those who are met wear what does duty as a veil—a light coat of some kind, generally of green silk, sleeves and all, which is cast over the head, and when men are met is drawn tightly over the face, so that only the eyes, sometimes only one eye, perhaps not even so much as that, can be seen; and often the wearer is so exceedingly bashful that she not only takes this precaution, but also turns her back to the street and her face to the wall of the houses along the way. But whenever I met a female thus coy and bashful, I always felt that one thing would surely happen,—that as soon as she thought I was fairly past, her curiosity would get the better of her bashfulness, and she would throw off all restraint, to see how the foreign stranger was dressed. Accordingly, after

SECLUSION OF WOMEN. 55

passing her a few steps, I would, if feeling a little mischievous, cast a quick glance over my shoulder, and catch the lady, generally with her face entirely exposed, in the act of gazing with both her eyes at the foreigner in his queer garb. Of course my glance back would disconcert her, and send her scurrying off in the opposite direction.

The cardinal point of social etiquette is that the ladies of a household are not to be seen, and, so far as conversation about them is concerned, are not supposed to exist. Consequently, when a visitor makes a call on a friend, he is not taken in and introduced to the wife or wives and daughters of his host. The guest-room and reception-rooms are either apart from the house or in front of the host's own residence. In the latter case no windows or doors look in upon the inner court or toward the women's apartments. The visitor is met in the front by his host, is there entertained, and in his conversation does not, unless he is a near relation or on the closest terms of intimacy, allude to the ladies of the house.

So, too, the institution which passes among us under the homely name of "courting" is not known in Corea. A young man there does not choose the partner of his joys and the sharer of his woes, nor does the young woman have a voice in the selection of a husband. She may have caught a glimpse of him through a hole in the window as he passed along the street, but he never knows how she looks, except from the description of his mother or other female relation, till he sees her on the wedding-day. The arrangement is a family matter, managed by the father. The method is somewhat as follows:—

A father, his son having reached a marriageable age —fourteen to sixteen—decides that the latter ought to settle down. Accordingly, he runs over the list of his acquaintances whom he knows to have marriageable daughters, and decides upon the family to which he will make overtures. Having got so far, he may talk the matter over with his wife, and having found her acquiescent, he will rise some morning, don his best apparel, and saunter down the street. The word "saunter" is used advisedly, for a Corean is seldom in a hurry. The old proverb so much quoted among Occidentals, "Never put off till to-morrow what you can do to-day," takes another shape in the Corean mind. It would probably run thus if it were formulated: "If a thing is not done to-day—why, there are other days coming; and if there should not be another day, it doesn't matter any way." Consequently, the father saunters leisurely along, saluting his acquaintances, stopping to discuss this matter or that, till he reaches the home of his friend. There he is welcomed by his host, who, noting the holiday garb, has probably surmised the object of the visit. Westerners would probably come immediately to the purpose in mind, but not so the Corean. He will talk on every subject but the one which is uppermost in his mind: prices, the last famine, the cholera, the feats of foreign ships of war, the state of the market, all may come under discussion. And when there is a lull in the conversation, the remark may fall, as if casually: "By the way, I have a son, a good-for-nothing fellow, whom I want to see settled in life." "Ah, is that so?" says the host. "I hope you will have the satisfaction of seeing him well married and a suitable wife attending to his wants." Then the conversation wanders off on any topic that suggests itself. After more or less time, if the host thinks favourably of what is in fact (and is so understood) a proposal, he will perhaps be heard to remark, "Do you know, it seems like a providence your coming here to-day! It just happens that I have a marriageable daughter, and perhaps you were directed here. Mayhap my daughter, who is a no-account girl, might be taught her duty to your son." And from that the two fathers may proceed to make the arrangements, after which the visitor goes home and tells his son that a wife has been found for him, and that he will be married on such a date. Visits are now in order between the women of the two families, and the details are arranged, and of course the mother tells her son the appearance of his bride, expatiating on her good points—her modesty, beauty, docility, obedience, and so on. The young man now takes a step upward in the social scale. He is now becoming a man, so he no longer wears his hair down his back in a braid, but has a little place shaved at the crown, and the rest of his hair done up in a knot on the top. He may now wear the black hat, and begin to assume the deliberate step and dignified manners of an adult. He must now be addressed in honorific language. He may talk to his boy companions of yesterday as inferiors. He is now a " Mr.," and is to be treated with becoming respect.

After the marriage the girl is carried to her husband's home in a closed chair with a leopard or tiger skin covering it, and takes her place in his family. She no longer has any ties connecting her with her own parents' home. She is part and parcel of the family into which she has married, and her hopes and ambitions are henceforth all in this direction.

Though women may not appear in the street by day, there is a time when they may take their outing. After the curfew strikes, all males are supposed to be in their homes, and the ladies may then go abroad. They do so in general, but still the coat is worn over the head; and by day or night the women are grotesque figures, with their full skirts, and with the sleeves of the coat flapping derisively from about the locality of the ears. At this time a foreigner walking through the streets will meet many a little company of women chatting along on their way to make a call.

If a call has to be made by a lady in the daytime, there is a great deal of trouble about it. She will be carried in a two-man chair, which may be de-

WEST GATE OF SEOUL.

scribed as a box rather less than three feet square and a trifle over three feet high, carried by two poles which run through rings in the sides of the bottom framework. This is enclosed by curtains, and a lady's chair is covered with little brass and ribbon ornaments which mark it as a lady's conveyance, and so warn off curious or prying glances. When a lady wishes to go out, one of the servants is sent to summon chair-coolies with their chair. They carry this into the inner court, set it down facing the entrance, and then retire. After they have gone, my lady's maid comes out, sees that no eyes are prying around, and then gives the signal for her mistress, who comes out, squats in front of the chair (which is too low for her to creep into), and shuffles back inside, to sit tailor-fashion on the bottom; the curtains are then carefully pulled down and examined to see that no cranny is left through which a prying eye can see the occupant; then the coolies are called in, given their directions, and they take up the chair and fare, and carrying her to the appointed place, set her down in the inner courtyard, retiring until she is ready to return, when the operation is repeated. It should be stated, however, that while the chair-curtains are so arranged as to prevent people's looking in, they do not prevent the occupant from seeing out, so that whatever goes on outside can be watched by my lady as she passes through the streets.

The labours of a woman in Corea lie in much

the same direction as in Great Britain. She is queen of the kitchen and laundry. She is seamstress and tailor, and she varies the monotony of her existence by embroidering in silk the badges of rank of her husband. The *cuisine* of the Corean is very limited. Rice is the staple, and that in a boiled state. Soup is common. Meat is not so common as with us, and when used is generally broiled.

Cooking occupies only a small part of the Corean wife's time. Her most wearying and incessant labour is at the laundry. Washing is done at the well-side, by the side of the street, or by the side of a brook or river. In a hollow in the brook's bed they dip the clothes, and then, laying them on a smooth stone, proceed to beat out the marks of wear, turning the cloth now and again to bring uncleansed spots under the paddle. They beat in time, as though to a tune, and dexterously change the paddle from one hand to the other without losing a stroke. Nowhere is there a more glowing whiteness produced in the laundry. Starch made of rice is used. Especially interesting is their method of ironing. In the first place, the "irons" are made of wood, and, instead of being flat, are round. The table, instead of being a flat board, is a wooden roller. They do not heat the "irons," but instead sometimes heat the flat stone on which the "ironing-board" rests. Instead of steady pressure to smooth out the wrinkles, the ironing is done by quick, sharp raps, like those of a drummer.

SEWING AND EMBROIDERY.

It is not unusual to see a woman in the field assisting in the gathering of the crops, and often in preparing them for use; but far less outdoor work is done by Corean women than by their sisters in Japan.

In sewing the women are very neat. They are extremely deliberate. Not much is accomplished in a day, but what is done is well done. As embroiderers, Coreans are not particularly skilful. In embroidery everything is stereotyped. The way of representing rocks is repeated in each piece of work. While in the representation of birds, bats, and butterflies they are wonderfully true to nature, and in reproducing such striking figures as the bamboo and various flowers they are accurate, the general effect of their work is tame and uninteresting.

CHAPTER VII.

MANNERS AND CUSTOMS.—(*Continued.*)

ONE tradition which obtains in Corea undoubtedly obstructs the advance of the country. It is that men of the *yang-ban* (gentleman or noble) class, even though their means do not furnish them with the necessities of life, must not work to make their own living. A gentleman may starve or beg, but may not work. His relations may support him, or his wife may, in one way or another, supply means, but he must not soil his hands.

When we arrived in Corea to begin our work at the king's school, called the Royal College, we found ourselves occupying an enviable position in Corean eyes, as men who had taken rank in a great foreign *quaga*. In other words, we were looked upon as "gentlemen" in the Corean sense, and were expected to keep up the dignity of our position. Now, Corean "gentlemen" are not supposed to carry anything for themselves. Even our scholars, who were all chosen from the nobility, would not carry their books from their studies to the class-rooms; a servant

ABSURD NOTIONS.

had to do that for them. Whenever a gentleman goes abroad, he is accompanied by a band of servants, more or less numerous according to his rank or means, who carry his belongings. He does not carry even his pipe. So when we went out into the street, it was very much against the will of our attendants that we should carry anything.

Soon after our arrival, a soldier was sent to each teacher, by order of His Majesty, to be a sort of personal attendant and messenger. If either of us went hunting, the soldier in attendance always took the gun, and carried it till we got to the hunting-grounds. The distress of my man was rather pitiful when once I brought out two pieces, a shot-gun and a rifle, so that he had to submit to my carrying one of them.

In like manner, in the spring, when one of the teachers commenced gardening, of which occupation he was especially fond, and began by using the spade, an attendant ran up and tried to take the spade out of his hands, remonstrating with him for doing "coolies' work."

Yet, in spite of such absurd prejudices, there is in Corea nothing resembling the caste distinctions of India. Men may pass, through the medium of scholarship, from the peasant class to the rank of scholar and noble. But there is a great deference among the people toward officials. For instance, in discussing business, men below a certain grade (that known as *cham-way*) may not sit in the presence of men of higher rank, unless invited to do so. Officials passing along the street are often preceded by soldiers and attendants, who clear the way for these great men, and order all men to rise and show respect to them. In the case of men of high rank, soldiers of a certain class precede the chair of the official by nearly a hundred yards, shouting out at short intervals, at the top of their voices, what sounds like "Kee-roo-che-roo-oo-oo! Kee-roo-che-roo-oo-oo!" Generally two old soldiers perform this duty, each taking his turn in shouting the above call. The exact translation of the term I have never learned, but the meaning is unmistakable. It is equivalent to "Look out, all you people! here comes a great man; get out of the way, and be prepared to show respect." After these two leading soldiers, who walk on opposite sides of the street, come others, sometimes to the number of thirty or forty, and they are followed, in the case of military officers, by two or more ranks of soldiers with muskets and fixed bayonets enclosing the chair of the officer, and then comes a train of servants, secretaries, etc., bearing various utensils.

Etiquette is graded with exactest nicety. Even the distance a host accompanies his guest on the latter's departure is measured by the elevation the guest has attained in official station. A curious custom is that two intimate friends passing along the street on horseback will not speak or recognize each

"CARDS OF IDENTIFICATION." 67

other. When a Corean riding in a chair meets in the street a foreigner whom he knows, he usually stops his chair, dismounts, and passes the time of day. This is a mark of respect, and a tribute not usually paid by Coreans to men of their own nationality.

Each male Corean carries with him a card of identification in the shape of a small piece of wood, on which are stamped his name and address. The possession of this "card" is obligatory. Many a time I have endeavoured to buy one of them, but was never successful—a pretty conclusive proof of their importance. One of our own men, when asked why he would not part with his, explained the reason in a graphic way: "If this were gone—" completing his unfinished sentence by drawing his finger around his neck and shrugging his shoulders, to represent decapitation. He may have been playing on my credulity, but there was probably some foundation for his statement.

Among the strange features of Corean life are the *changs* or fairs, where the trade of the country is carried on. The places for these fairs are always near a stream and close to cross-roads, and of course on a level spot. These spots are marked by a few inns and by rude sheds, put up for the protection of the wares. The fairs are held about every five days, and on fair days what at other times looks like a deserted village becomes lively with the moving crowds and resonant with the cries of the vendors. The goods are displayed under a shed or in the open air, and often a huge umbrella will shelter the stock in trade of a merchant. As the fairs are held on different days in different districts, vendors move from one to another, transporting on their own backs or on those of oxen or ponies the stock remaining unsold at the last one. It has arisen from this custom that there is a profession of peddlers and another of porters, and these peddlers are organized into a guild which goes by the name of *pusang*. The porters are also organized, and they are called *posang*. The former guild is under government protection and supervision; it is divided into sections of one thousand men, with heads or chiefs appointed by the home office. These men are utilized by the government in various ways. They serve, for example, as detectives, their roving life making them of much value in this way, and they are also liable for military service. They are said to number nearly one hundred and fifty thousand men, and their patriotism is of a very high order.

The following graphic description is given by Mr. Foulk, attaché to the United States legation at Seoul. It tells his experience in returning from a visit to Song-To, a stronghold and one of the fortresses of the capital.

"It was nightfall when we started to return. The magistrate, who was an officer of the *pusang*, brought his seal into use, and called out thirty of the body to light us down the mountains. Where these men came from, or how they were called, I did not understand, for we were apparently in an uninhabited, wild mountain district. They appeared quickly, great, rough mountain-men, each wearing a straw hat with a cotton ball in the band, and the characters 'fidelity' and 'loyalty' written on the brim. We descended the worst ravine in a long, weird, winding procession, the mountains and our path weirdly illuminated by the pine torches of the *pusang* men, who uttered shrill reverberating cries continually to indicate the road or each other's whereabouts. Suddenly we came upon a little pavilion in the darkest part of the first gorge; here some two hundred more *pusang* men were assembled by a wild stream in the light of many bonfires and torches. On the call of the magistrate they had prepared a feast for us here at midnight in the mountains. The magistrate told me that he had been asked by the late minister to the United States, Nim Yong Ik, to suddenly call on the *pusang* men of the Song-To district for services, to show me the usefulness and fidelity of the body; and he had selected this place, the middle of the mountains, and time, the middle of the night. I need not say that the experience was wonderful and impressive. The manner of the magistrate to the *pusang* men was most kind and pleasing, and they likewise exhibited the utmost regard and deference for him. I was assigned the place of honour at the feast—in the middle—before the largest table, which was piled with a great variety of food. The leading *pusang* men—old men, nicely dressed, with kind faces—were presented to me, and exhibited curiously their pleasure in thus talking pleasantly with a foreigner for the first time in their lives. The fact of my travelling in Corea utterly alone (so far as the company of other foreigners was concerned) seemed to please them very much.

"In returning to the city our own escort was sent to the rear at the request of the *pusang* men, who took charge of us. They carried us across rocky streams, up and down rocky gullies, energetic and cheerful all the while, a distance of eight miles, thence on into the city over a comparatively level road. Thirty or forty men carried torches, *which were found lying across the path* at regular intervals, to light the way. At 3 A.M. we arrived at the *yongnmu* (official residence); here the *pusang* men were dismissed, to return, for the most part, to their homes in the mountains."

Many little customs of the Coreans strike a foreigner as odd: for instance, hats are not removed by visitors when they enter a house, nor in greeting an acquaintance on the street; but the shoes, which resemble our slippers, are left at the door when a call is made. The Corean language is written not in words but by syllables. It can, therefore, be written so as to be read intelligently either up or down, or from left to right, or *vice versa*. The usual way of writing, and the only way of printing, however, is in vertical columns, beginning at the right. Often the greeting and name of the writer come first. The people sit down at their work much more than we do. A woman sits to wash and iron, a carpenter sits to plane and saw, and a labourer to chop wood. The method of counting on the hands is peculiar. All the fingers are closed. One extends the thumb, two the forefinger, and so on; then six closes the little finger, seven the third finger, and so on; while eleven extends the thumb, and so on. As in China, the last name comes first; so that if a man's name is written Kim Chul Mo, he is Mr. Kim. But he is not addressed in that way; he is called "Kim So-Pang," "Kim Mr." So all titles follow the family name. Hence a gentleman is not called "Count Min," but "Min Count." In reviews the cavalry is drawn up with the tails of the horses to the street. When the four quarters of the compass are mentioned, it is in the order east, west, south, north. So points between are not "south-east," "north-west," but "east-south," "west-north." The farmer's plough throws the furrows to the left. The saws for making planks and boards have their teeth pointed away from the centre toward the ends, instead of all pointing the one way. In fractions, the denominator comes first; not "three-fourths," but "fourths-three," is the order. In entertainments, the place of honour is at the left of the host. The seasons are in the same order, but the first three months are spring, the next summer, and so on, irrespective of temperature and the sun's course in the heavens.

CHAPTER VIII.

FASHIONS.

AN Englishman was once heard to say that the dirtiest man he ever saw was a clean Corean, and visitors to the country would generally agree with him. It can only be said by way of excuse for the people of the peninsula, that their white summer clothing is very easily soiled, while their thick-quilted winter garments are troublesome to wash.

The fabrics of which clothes are made in Corea are cotton, silks, and grass cloths; no woollen garments are found there.

The prevailing colour of clothing is white. But the cotton is, for women, often dyed blue; for boys and girls, red or pink. The silks are of all colours except black, and the gaudiest materials are used by the men. Black is used only in the hat. The play of colour on a Corean street, especially when viewed from an eminence, is very varied and bright.

One of the first matters of concern in the toilet of these people is the hair. Boys wear all their hair down their backs in a braid. This must not be con-

THE HAIR. 73

founded with the queue of the Chinese. The Chinaman shaves all the hair except that on the crown; the Corean boy has all his hair braided. As soon as a boy is betrothed or married, he becomes a man, and the transition is shown in the style of dressing the hair. His hair is unbraided, a spot as large as a crown piece is shaved on the top of his head, and all the hair is then combed up toward a spot about two inches from the top of the forehead, and there gathered into a "top-knot." This knot is about two inches high, and sticks up from the head like a little blunt horn. The next operation is the binding on of the *mangon*. This is a band about an inch and a half wide, of woven horse-hair, which is bound around the forehead. It is drawn tightly around the head and tied behind. Once a boy puts this on he is a man.

The women dress their hair in a very neat fashion by parting it in the middle, then combing it straight back and coiling it low on the back of the neck. Through this coil a pin is thrust to hold it in place.

The articles of clothing commonly worn are a hat; a tunic, loose and reaching to the waist; loose, baggy trousers supported by a girdle and gathered in at the knee by leggings which tie at the ankles; stockings padded with cotton; and over all a coat, the sleeves of which are wide-flowing and reach to the hips or lower, and are sewed up from the bottom to the wrist so as to form very capacious pockets. Not to be forgotten are the purse for coins, the knife and the tobacco pouch and pipe, with flint and tinder or matches, without which no Corean is dressed. The use of tobacco is universal, even boys and women using the weed.

A traveller has well said that you can tell approximately the rank of a Corean by noting the length of his pipe stem. The official is unable to light his pipe by holding a match to it—he cannot reach the bowl. So men of rank have their pipes filled and lighted by their servants. Much taste is displayed in the ornamentation of the pipes. The bowls are usually of metal, and the mouth-pieces are often of the same material. The most expensive mouth-pieces are made of jade. Short and handy pipes of foreign make are coming into use among the coolies, but a short pipe is to a man of note an abomination.

Of all lands in the world, Corea is the land of hats, and leads the world in the superficial area of head-gear. Hats may be seen measuring over two feet from rim to crown. The usual hat is of black woven horse-hair. Often not merely one hat is worn at a time, but sometimes three together. First there is the *mangon*, then another indicating that the wearer has "taken the *quaga*" or passed an examination for the rank of "scholar," and over these the usual straight-brimmed black hat. At the palace, the outside hat is discarded, and instead of the *quaga* hat, one of similar shape is used, but with two appendages looking like little wings joining at the back and stretching round loosely to just above the ears. These ear-tabs let loose are said to typify the ear of the servants and courtiers open to the commands of the king. His Majesty wears the same kind of a hat, but in his case the ear-tabs are tied up, as of course there is no one to issue commands to him.

In Corea, as in China, it is a mark of respect to keep on the hat in the presence of others. It is said that so peculiar and so nicely settled is the way of wearing the hat, that the rank of high officials can be told by the set of the head-gear; it being, in the words of a native, "not too much *so*, nor too much *so*."

The coats are made in several shapes. One is very much like the full-dress evening coat, with the tails greatly lengthened. Another is like an exaggerated sack coat with the flowing sleeves already mentioned.

The colour of these is often white; for boys, especially those who are engaged to be married, pink; sometimes a pale blue is the shade, and not seldom green. Often two or three coats made of silks of different colours are worn at once, the effect sometimes being very pretty, often very odd. The winter overcoat is made of the same materials, but is padded with cotton and quilted. Those worn by the wealthy are often trimmed, and occasionally lined, with fur of sable or mink. For winter wear, the tunic and trousers also are padded and quilted, so that people endure well the severe cold of their steady winter.

The dress of women differs only slightly from that

above described. They use the same shoes, wooden and leather, as the men, the same padded stockings, the same trousers and leggings, but over them a full skirt generally coloured blue (girls usually wear pink), and falling below the knee.

Most of the women seen in the streets are models of neatness, their shoes, stockings, skirts, and leggings shining like incrusted snow in the sunshine. They are fond of adornment, and are skilled in the use of powder to whiten the skin. They wear not one wedding-ring but two, and these of silver, very thick and massive.

The most peculiar article of woman's wear is the coat worn over the head. This is made of green or blue cloth or silk.

Mention should not be omitted of the court-dress of officials, which, in addition to the items already described, consists of a dark-green overcoat, on the back and breast of which is worn a square of cloth upon which figures are embroidered. These figures are either cranes or tigers, the former denoting civil rank, the latter military. All officials below a certain grade may wear only one of these figures; all above that grade wear two. In addition to these signs of rank, there is another, worn on the *mangon* behind the ear.

One thing that strikes foreigners is the universal use of the fan. A part of the equipment even of soldiers is a large fan. Every person who keeps

FANS.

servants is supposed to supply them during the summer season with these indispensable articles; and they serve not only to cool the person, but also to shield the face from too curious observers. Many a time have we passed Coreans on horseback and been amused to see the riders hold their fans before their faces so as not to be seen.

In summer Coreans have a peculiar device for keeping cool. Next the body is worn a framework made of split bamboo woven in fancy designs. This is so made that it is supported from the shoulders and springs out from the body. It therefore holds the tunic away from the person, and permits the air to penetrate beneath the clothing and circulate freely.

CHAPTER IX.

PLEASURES AND SOLEMNITIES.

COREANS are fond of fun. From the small toddler who can scarcely stand, to the gray-haired minister of state, all like fun, and do their share in making it. Going through the streets of the city or along the country roads, one will find much the same diversity of games as is seen in our own land, and each game has its appropriate season.

By far the most popular amusement is kite-flying. To fly the Corean kite involves an amount of skill far exceeding that called for by the English species. The name given to kites is *yun*, and they are of peculiar construction. They are nearly square, constructed of thin pieces of bamboo covered with tough paper, with a hole left in the centre, and connected with the line by three pieces of string joined to the sides near the top and to the centre of the bottom. A nice degree of skill and practice is required so to attach the line as to make the kite balance. It generally has no tail, and is therefore very unsteady in its movements, until a great amount of line is out.

ENTRANCE TO THE PALACE.

"KITE-FIGHTS."

Men and boys of all ages indulge in the pastime. The "kite-fights" are an absorbing part of the sport. The object of each of the combatants in these fights is either to haul down his adversary's kite by entangling the lines, or to saw through the one line with the other, and cause the loss of the kite. The kites dash and curvet in the air, and dive and plunge at each other in such a way as easily to suggest to the imagination that they are alive.

To witness a kite-fight the shopkeeper will often stop serving a customer and risk losing a sale, though, as a rule, the customer is as eager as any one to see the fun. So great is the interest in these encounters, that sometimes a thousand people gather and look on in breathless excitement, and with keenest interest, which they show by their ejaculations and cries of encouragement or dismay, as one or the other of the combatants scores a point or wins the game.

In the winter and early spring, favourite amusements are jumping the rope and see-saw. Pitching coins is another popular game with young and old. Many a time a little knot may be seen collected around two boys who are the champions of their districts engaged in settling a dispute as to their skill in tossing. Boys may also be seen whipping tops along the streets.

One of the most common Corean words is *koogyung*, sight-seeing. The people are exceedingly fond of spectacles. Accordingly, whenever the king and prince leave the palace for an outing, or for purposes of worship, or on other occasions, the day is a holiday; the opportunity is seized for making a display, and the people gather to witness the sights.

The show or *kur-dong* is coming! Coolies are carrying baskets of soil, which they strew down the middle of the streets through which the king is to pass. The tradition is that His Majesty's person is sacred, and he must not be carried over soil trodden by the foot of common man. Virgin soil must be beneath his royal soles.

At last comes the procession: companies of soldiers of varied sorts—footmen and cavalry, spearmen, swordsmen, and bowmen—leading the way; captains and generals, guarded by files of soldiers, each one held on his horse by men on either side of him, and the horse led by a groom. The little horses are tipped out with brass-bedecked coverings. Officials are in their most gorgeous robes. Flags stream in the wind. Men armed with poles pass along the sides of the street, pushing or striking the people with the poles to keep the way clear, and sometimes singling out some unfortunate individual for severe punishment in this way. Now comes a body of tiger-hunters, bearing the native match-lock or flint-lock weapons—men to whom fear is said to be unknown; who else dare beard the royal man-eater in his lair? Clad as they are in flowing and picturesque uniforms of blue, with dark, broad-

THE ROYAL PROCESSION.

brimmed hats adorned with red tassels, they present a striking appearance. It may be that right behind them marches, in company front, a regiment of infantry, armed with breech-loading Remingtons and sabre bayonets, and dressed in what are supposed to be foreign-fashioned uniforms. The generals look ridiculously helpless, supported by their attendants, and they are said to go into battle held on their horses. Civil officers are attended by huge retinues of servants; and one of the novel sights is an official who, instead of being carried in a chair on the shoulders of men, rides a unicycle, the seat being over the wheel. The official is held up by servants on each side, while the motive power is furnished by coolies, who push and pull at poles passed through the bottom of the chair or seat. One has fair time to get wearied watching troop after troop of cavalry, mounted on ridiculously small horses, company after company of infantry armed with medieval or modern weapons, bodies of spearmen and clubmen and swordsmen, companies of bowmen and others, before the noise made by a company of buglers announces the approach of the king. Before the king is always carried a large chair borne by eighteen men, with no one in it. This chair is exactly like the one His Majesty occupies. The custom originated in the times when the king was always carried in a closed chair. Once when the monarch was going out a conspiracy had been formed, and through the chair which was supposed to contain him arrows were shot with the purpose of assassinating him. But he happened to be in another chair, and so escaped. Ever since that occasion an empty chair has been borne in the royal procession, and as long as closed ones were used it was not known in which one the king rode. But since the ruler of the kingdom began to ride in open chairs, the custom has been maintained, simply as a reminiscence of the ancient attempt at regicide. The king himself is borne in a large open chair raised aloft in the air; for none may look down upon His Majesty. He is in full view of all who choose to look, though the natives are accustomed to bow the head as he passes. To foreigners, when present in a body, he almost always shows the courtesy of stopping the chair a moment as he passes. If during an outing he passes foreigners to whom he has granted audience, and even others whom he knows only by reputation, he generally recognizes them by a gracious bow and a very pleasant smile. After him is usually carried a second empty chair, and following that comes one which bears the prince, who generally accompanies his father. After them go other bodies of soldiers—nearly a repetition of what precedes.

I know of no procession in which the display of colour is so varied and magnificent as in the Corean capital on the day of the king's outing. The varied suits of the troops, the gorgeous standards and flags embroidered with silks, the gay trappings of the horses, and the brilliant clothing of the courtiers, flanked by the gala dress of the natives, make a kaleidoscopic picture probably not to be equalled elsewhere in the world, unless perhaps in India. These shows are good opportunities for the king to exhibit himself to the populace, and keep himself in their favour. As he goes out four or five times a year, he succeeds in maintaining his popularity, and at the same time, by being unapproachable by the masses except at such times, the "majesty which doth hedge a king" is easily supported, and with it the awe of the common people for the august ruler of the kingdom, the "favourite of Heaven."

Another spectacle, which reminds one of the mystery or miracle plays of England, collects crowds of people in places where the hollows in the hillsides form natural theatres. The players, in hideous masks, personate legendary and mythical characters, and the performance lasts for two or three days. The object of these it seems difficult to learn, and, curiously enough, they are not visited by the mandarins or gentlemen of the vicinity. They seem to be frowned upon by the orthodox Confucian. No collection is taken up, and no fee demanded.

But all the rage in the late winter and early spring is the game which stirs up the most life and engages the most zeal—the stone-fight. Villages are generally built around the bases or upon the sides of the rolling hills and spurs of the mountains. Often between two villages thus situated there is a large level stretch, and this is made an annual battle-ground. The sport usually begins in good-humour, often continues so to the end, but not unfrequently engenders bad blood, and arouses angry passions. The game is begun by the boys, sometimes early in the afternoon, and there is desultory fighting until towards evening. Then the men begin to arrive and take a hand, and the battle becomes sharp. The end comes soon after sunset. The weapons employed are stones and clubs, the stones being thrown from the hand or from slings made of straw string. Sometimes these stone-fights become more than mere sport, and are the occasions when the bad blood existing between the villages is let out. Occasionally, so large are the numbers engaged, so great the noise made, and so dangerous to life is the game, that the thing comes to the king's ears, and he has to give orders that the fighting shall cease. It is a wonder that so few are hurt; but when we remember that the participants wear their winter clothes, including a long, flowing overcoat padded with cotton, the danger is seen to be much less than at first seems to be the case. A traveller who visits Corea and does not see one of these fights, misses one of the most characteristic sights to be witnessed among this strange people.

The Coreans are exceedingly fond of singing. Most

of their songs are exceedingly monotonous, reminding one of the chants of the medieval monks. A single note is held and dwelt on, and harmony is unknown. Corean music has but the air. Even a bass is unknown. The consequence is that a foreign band appears to the people to emit a jargon of sounds. But on the few occasions when a band of musicians from a war-vessel has visited the capital, crowds of people have gathered to listen, and quaint and queer are the comments dropped at such times.

The favourite musical instrument of the Coreans is a compound of the clarionet and the cornet, the mouth-piece and stem being of reed and bamboo, and the flare or end of brass. At dinners "music" is furnished by a band, but upon Western ears the impression is decidedly unpleasant. The instruments are Chinese in origin, are very imperfect, and the music is in a minor key.

Dancing, too, is a favourite pastime, the dancing, however, being rather posturing according to the Japanese or nautch-girl fashion. These gestures being wavy motions of the arms and hands and sinuous twistings of the body, accompanied by slow though comely slides, are very graceful.

The solemnities of Coreans are confined to the thought of the dead. Yet they do not seem to dread death, for their belief leads them to look for a life beyond. While Heaven is angry when it removes a friend or relation who has not reached old age, it is the survivors who are punished, not the one whom death has taken away.

Hills are the burial-places. Passing out of the capital by almost any road, the traveller will come upon the burying-places, always on the tops and sides of hills and bold knolls, never in the valleys. The social position held by the deceased can always be inferred from the size of the mound over the grave and the amount of space devoted to it. For members of the royal family a single grave occupies a hill, and no one else is interred there. Of wealthy men or high officials, several may occupy a hill together. But the people are buried together in numbers, their graves as closely contiguous as they can be placed.

A Corean funeral is a sad affair. When a death occurs in any family, the neighbours have no excuse for being ignorant of the fact. The women and girls and boys mourn in shrill and penetrating tones, that reverberate through the night air with frightful distinctness. Oftentimes hired mourners are called in, and they make night hideous with their cries.

It is probably on account of the occupation of the hills as burial-grounds, and the horror felt at the thought of disturbing graves, that the Coreans are averse to opening up the mineral wealth lying in the mountains. As worship is paid to the spirits of the dead at the graves, disturbing the tombs is to the people the equivalent of sacrilege.

CHAPTER X.

RELIGIONS AND SUPERSTITIONS.

RELIGION in Corea has not attained the intensity of growth which it has reached in China and Japan.

The temples are few, and lack the element of picturesqueness. They reflect the poverty of the country. Stately structures on commanding sites, approached through rows of votive lanterns, rich in lacquer and wealthy in decorations and gifts, are conspicuous only by their absence.

While China and Japan have each three cults or forms of religion, in Corea only two are found—Buddhism and Confucianism. Of course the introduction of both of these was from China.

From the lowest peasant up to the king, Confucianism has been long practised by all. There are traces throughout the country of a former more extensive worship of Buddha; but at present, while not tabooed, Buddhism is little followed. True, the guardians of some of the fortresses are Buddhist monks. They are supported by His Majesty from the public granaries in return for this service. The monks who have the care of the little shrines placed here and there along the road do not have this advantage, but they beg from the people, and certainly do not seem to suffer. There is no mutilation, no maiming of the body, nothing that repels one from the priests and monks except the shaving of the head. Yet the status of Buddhism in the eyes of the people is fixed by the fact that no monk may enter the capital. If one is found there he is put to death. Nor are there any temples inside the walls of the capital. There are ancestral tablets before which Confucian rites are performed, but nothing like a temple except one in the north-west corner of the city, a "Temple of Heaven"—really no temple at all, but an open space paved and surrounded by a low wall, and with a grove as a background.

One who visits, say, the fortress of Puk Hon, some ten miles to the north of the capital, will find the men inside it all monks. He will see these men with shaved heads lounging about, doing nothing that looks at all like either military or religious duty, except that a number may be found at a dingy temple, in which are disreputable images, before which attendants mumble or chant prayers unintelligible even to themselves. Diligent inquiry would show that these monks are not such upon deep conviction and from religious principle, but that the rice given from the public stores suffices to make this mode of living

VILLAGE IDOLS.

SPIRITS AND DEMONS. 93

attractive to them. Among the people I never met a single hearty Buddhist. I found persons who spoke of the monks with a laugh or a sneer, showing in their way of speaking that they pitied them. The monks themselves are harmless enough. They seem too lazy to do anything. They are in a state of harmless inactivity.

The real worship of the Coreans is before the ancestral tablets and at the graves. It is simple in character. It consists merely of setting out on small tables offerings, principally rice with various condiments, before which prostrations are made and prayers offered. The spirit is supposed to be present, and to partake of the gifts thus presented.

But subsidiary to these two religions, which are the prominent religious features, is a belief in a multiplicity of spirits and demons of different powers and various characters. The gates of the cities, palaces, temples, and often of private houses, are surmounted by grotesque shapes of animals and contorted figures of men. These are to frighten off the various spirits of evil and the demons, which otherwise might enter the city to disturb its peace and destroy its prosperity. During the cholera season of 1886, as I passed from street to street, I often found stretched across the entrances of the narrower ways bits of string from which hung slips of paper or pieces of rag inscribed with invocations to cholera devils not to enter that street and carry off the inhabitants. Fires were burned outside the walls to scare away or propitiate the same malicious beings. As the traveller goes along any road or path, he will every little while pass a tree or bush decorated with bits of coloured rag or paper; occasionally a prayer is attached, and beneath the tree will be found an irregular pile of small stones. He will find that these bushes or trees are the reputed homes of sprites or genii, and that the stones are cast there by chance wayfarers, who hope to deposit with the stones whatever bad luck the journey may have brought them.

Here and there the tourist may be shown a little hut, inside of which he will find some figures painted on paper, representing a patron deity, and hung on the walls prayers in Corean and Chinese, in which the petitioner begs " for one year of three hundred and sixty days to be delivered from all sorts of sickness and disease, and from all unprofitable ventures." Occasionally a more stately building will be seen, which is perhaps erected to the memory of some celebrated warrior, in whose honour the temple was built. In the building will probably be found the figure of the deified warrior, in red and gilt, with glaring eyes and impossible moustache, seated in defiant attitude on his throne. In close proximity to each other may be seen the strangest objects— gifts of worshippers. An ancient sword of native make keeps guard, while a Waterbury clock ticks the seconds as if in derision. In one shrine I saw before the god a solitary rubber boot, much the worse for wear, which the donor had perhaps picked up from the ash-heap of some foreign resident of the capital.

Not long after my arrival in Corea, I was startled by one of the men attached to the house running in to tell me, with an air of perturbation, that a heavenly dog was eating up the moon, and would I please come out and see? It occurred to me that there was an eclipse of the moon due at that time, so I went out to view the phenomenon. When I got out of the house I heard a great din in the street, the beating of drums and iron instruments throughout the city, together with firing of guns. Soon came from the palace the sound of platoon firing, and then the quick rattle of Gatling guns turned on the voracious monster. Asking what all this meant, I was told that it was noise made with the object of scaring off the heavenly dog; that it had been uniformly successful all through Corean history; that though the beast had often nearly eaten the moon up, he had always been scared away before completing it; and, in short, that this noise was very good medicine, and that they proposed to keep it up.

Bodily ailments are ascribed to the evil influences of sprites and devils. The exorcists and conjurers find in the commonest of them excuses for using their powers in dispossessing the sick body of the sprites which have made it their home. Their treatment is a noisy one. Day and night, it may be for a week, the ceaseless beat of drums is maintained, until nature is either wearied out and death results, or she recovers herself and the patient is restored to health.

One of the departments of the government is that of etiquette and ceremonies, in which men studied in magic and in the lore of omens regulate official and royal conduct, guiding the course of events according to tradition and to prognostications from chance happenings. That an event is unlucky is sufficient to forbid the entrance upon any enterprise.

Consequent upon this belief in omens are various subterfuges for circumventing Dame Fortune. Thus the season of kite-flying, which ends on the fifteenth day of the first moon, is closed by cutting the string of the kite as it flies in the air, when it falls and bears away with it much of the bad luck which might have attended the owner during the year. At the same season of the year, an effigy of straw, representing the maker, is tied together, and in different parts of it are hidden cash, and also a scrap of paper on which is written, in Corean or Chinese, some such prayer as, "For one year of twelve months, from all plagues and diseases and misfortunes deliver me." This effigy is then given to a boy who calls for it, and he, after cutting it up sufficiently to secure all the cash that can possibly be hidden in it, throws it down where roads cross or meet. Sometimes a number of these effigies accumulate at some cross-roads, and the bystanders amuse themselves by making a fire of them, or in kicking them about. The more this man of straw is mutilated, the better the luck of the person it represents, and the more complete his immunity from the evils that may assail him.

On this same day, it is the custom for men of the same station in life to call to each other as they pass along the street, and if one answers the other, the person answering is supposed to carry away in his own person whatsoever diseases and misfortunes might have befallen the one who accosted him. Therefore on that day every one is on his guard, and to the various and pressing calls no heed is given. On this day nearly all partake of one meal, in which five kinds of grain are used—this being a mode of beseeching an abundance and variety of food during the coming year. At this meal a peculiar kind of wine, called the "ear-brightening wine," is drunk, which is supposed to have the effect of sharpening the hearing and preventing aural diseases. At night there is a suspension of laws relating to curfew, and men may wander around the city without fear of arrest. The reason for this privilege is a current superstition that if a person traverse the city and pass over every bridge within the walls, he will have immunity from diseases of the lower limbs and extremities for a year. For this day nine is the lucky number.

Accordingly, nine meals are eaten. If a man bring to the house a load of wood, he must manage to bring nine; or if a woman spin, she must spin nine bundles. The fifteenth of the Corean January is the time for prognostications regarding weather and crops. If on that day there is any wind, there will be much wind during the spring. Men go down to the barley-fields and pull up grains of barley. If these grains have only one main root, the crop will be small; two roots denote a fair crop; while three foretell a great abundance. The wise ones also tell which months will be the most rainy. A piece of bamboo is split, and into the slit twelve beans are inserted, and the whole is taken into the field and buried lightly for the dew or rain to moisten. The beans which swell most represent the months in which there will be the greatest rainfall.

CHAPTER XI.

RESOURCES.

MEASURED by her developed industries, her exports and her imports, Corea is perhaps the poorest member of the family of nations. Not a twentieth part of the arable land is under cultivation. There are no manufactures which command an outside market, and though Corea has plenty of mineral wealth, what little is developed is done only in the crudest and most wasteful manner. The fisheries—another valuable source of income—are neglected. The northern and western parts of the peninsula are well wooded, and a large revenue might be made from the sale of the timber in Japan and China, yet no advantage is taken of the markets offered there.

As is the rule in the East, agriculture is on a small scale. Upland and lowland are cultivated, the latter for rice, the former for varied products. The area under cultivation is very small, but what land is tilled at all is well tilled.

The most striking agricultural implement is the shovel, the mode of working which is rather unusual.

This instrument has a straight handle about seven feet long, which is set into the blade, and this is made of wood, shod at the point and sides with iron. In the upper corners of the blade holes are bored and ropes are attached. One man takes the handle, holding it nearly perpendicularly and guiding it into the dirt, while one, two, or three men hold and pull each rope, throwing or carrying the soil where it is needed. Work can be done very rapidly in this way, and I have seen labourers throw earth to a distance of two rods with one of these shovels.

Of grains the principal is rice, and most of the valleys are taken advantage of for the culture of this cereal. In a sufficiently wet season there is a large quantity of rice raised, but never enough for the needs of the people. The deficiency is supplied from Japan. Barley is grown in moderate quantities, and is sometimes used as food by the poorer classes, but its principal use is as food for cattle. Wheat is very little known, though some is grown in the north and a little around the capital. A grain which is very useful to the people is millet, of which there are several varieties. This is one of the most graceful of cereals, and as it ripens, its heavy, well-filled head bowing gracefully on its strong stem and waving to the wind, it makes a very pretty picture.

The Coreans have a very ingenious way of keeping the sparrows and magpies from their grain-fields. Strings are stretched between posts right across the

WORKING WITH THE SHOVEL.

FRUITS AND VEGETABLES. 103

fields, and on them are hung scare-crows of rags. Boys are employed to watch the fields, and as the birds attempt to settle, they shake the stakes and strings, and shout with lusty lungs, thus keeping the little thieves from their pilferings. Three or four boys, with the assistance of the strings and stakes, and a man to look after them, can protect quite a large field from the depredations of the feathered robbers.

The foregoing list includes the principal resources of the inhabitants for food. Large granaries are placed in the principal cities and in the fortresses, in which the tribute rice is stored. In times of scarcity these granaries are sometimes opened for the benefit of the people. The real purpose, however, is to receive the tribute, which is paid in kind, and to afford sustenance for the army and for His Majesty's retainers.

In the way of fruits, a great variety is found in Corea. Apples, pears, peaches, apricots, plums, and many others, grow abundantly.

Vegetables, too, are very numerous, the most popular being potatoes, lettuce, and cucumbers. No one who has not visited Corea can realize how much this last production can be to a people. Many a meal of the Corean consists of nothing but a cucumber, eaten whole, skin and all!

Other agricultural products are cotton, of not very good quality, growing rather poor, and mulberry trees for the silk industry, found chiefly in the south.

104   BEASTS OF LABOUR AND BURDEN.

Corean silk is very thin, poorly spun, and not well woven. It resembles very thin pongee, and is not likely to become an article of commerce. Flax is also raised to some extent, and a fair quality of coarse linen is manufactured.

Ploughing is done with oxen or cows. The oxen are of enormous size, and the ordinary cattle one meets along the roads are larger than the average prize cattle of our own land. They are kept by the natives solely as beasts of labour and burden, for Coreans use neither butter nor milk. In a ride of a few miles in the morning, a person will meet hundreds of the patient beasts moving slowly along, almost entirely hidden beneath loads of grass or brushwood which is being taken into the city to be sold as fuel.

But if the oxen are of large size, the horses or ponies are equally small. Few of these animals measure fourteen hands. The consequence is, that a very tall foreigner has sometimes to hold his feet up when riding on a foreign saddle. The Coreans escape this difficulty by having their saddles built up nearly a foot from the horse's back. One of the ludicrous sights which met me on my first day in the country was one of these little animals running away with a tall foreigner on its back, his rider trying to stop the beast by dragging his feet along the ground, a course which eventually brought down both man and horse.

Of mineral wealth Corea has an abundance, but, as stated, it is undeveloped. In the neighbourhood of Ping Yang, the former capital, there are magnificent veins of coal, seemingly anthracite, and yet burning with almost the readiness of the bituminous variety. This coal is quite hard, burns out well, makes almost no smoke, and even the dust can be and is utilized when rolled into balls with a little wet clay. This coal-field, not, we believe, the only one in Corea, is worked as yet only by the Coreans, and that in a most wasteful manner. They simply grub out what is easiest to get at, tumble the rock and earth back into the excavation, and so cover up at least as valuable deposits as they excavate. The mines are almost on the bank of a large and navigable river, so that there seems no reason why the native article should not become a competitor with the Japanese, not only in Corea, but in all the markets of the East. Several good offers have been made by foreign firms, German and American, to open the mines and give the government a fair percentage of the proceeds, but these have always been refused. The government at one time decided to open up the mines themselves. Accordingly, mining machinery was bought; but it has never been erected, and is now scattered all over the country, rusting away, with many parts missing, which have been stolen for their value as old iron.

Not very far from these coal mines, iron ore of an

excellent quality is to be found. With abundant supplies of these two staples of industry almost touching each other, the statement that Corea may become wealthy is not unfounded.

The principal source of revenue to Corea at present is gold-dust. In obtaining this, too, the crudest methods are in vogue. Only a few placer diggings are worked, and yet a good many thousand pounds' worth of dust is said to be sent every year to Japan.

A considerable amount of silver is also gathered in different localities. Copper, too, is found in abundance, and is more used than any other metal.

The country has not yet been scientifically explored, but its geological formation is so varied that, in all probability, much that will enrich the little kingdom will yet be found stored away in her hills and woods.

The fisheries, which are excellent, produce no revenue for the kingdom, as the fishermen sell only to their own people. Immense quantities of fish are dried, and very queer are some of the ways for preserving them.

A few pearls are found, but very few of good shape and colour, most of them, though large, being flat and dark. They are highly esteemed among the people, and bring good prices from officials.

The last great invasion of the peninsula by the Japanese marks the death of Corean industry and art and the renaissance of Japanese art. The Japanese, when they retired, carried away with them every artisan from whom they were likely to learn anything, and so brought about a revival of industry and of production of art objects in their own country and the extinction of both in Corea. There cannot be claimed now for Corea any important manufacture. The two lines in which the most is done are cabinet-work and the production of brassware.

In the making of both brass-work and cabinets no originality is shown, and each piece is modelled after a pattern with great exactness. Every design seems to be stereotyped.

In the south some mother-of-pearl work is done which has a very pretty effect, and indeed a few pieces show great artistic taste.

Fans of various sizes, shapes, and materials are made in the country, and as tribute to His Majesty is paid in kind, he has a vast number to give as presents to his servants and to the nobles who have duties at the palace. These fans are far superior in strength to those of Japanese make, though the paper is pasted only on one side. The bamboo which forms the framework is well polished, and often decorated with great patience and pretty effect.

Another industry peculiar to Corea is the making of Kang-Wha mats. These are made at Kang-Wha, of rushes which are cultivated only there. The patterns, which look as though they were painted on, are really made of short pieces of stained rush *sewed* on, but so closely and carefully done that only the minutest examination reveals the secret of their make-up. These are not made even for domestic commerce, but are meant for His Majesty's use alone. But they find their way into the market through being presented at the palace to this or that mandarin, whence they pass for ready money into the merchant's hands.

Embroidery is continually being done in the palace, where a trained corps of women is kept for this purpose. They do work on silk for screen-panels, and though exceedingly conventional in their treatment of rocks, clouds, water, and landscape generally, their figures of birds, butterflies, bats, and the palm and bamboo are very correct and lifelike. I have seen very few Corean paintings, but to a Western eye they were exceedingly ridiculous, showing not even the most elementary knowledge of perspective. In the temples erected to the honour of deified heroes there are usually a number of paintings purporting to portray the important events and achievements in the lives of the heroes. These bear a very marked resemblance to similar paintings in Japan, the style of execution being the same.

In the foreign commercial relations there is as yet little inducement for foreigners to enter the country. Chinamen are there in great numbers, as also Japanese, who have opened shops where nearly everything of foreign production can be obtained. Since Chinese and Japanese can live very much cheaper than Western merchants, as a rule they can sell for much less, and consequently there is nothing to induce traders to settle there. Besides this, the poverty of the people is so great that they are unable to pay the high prices Western-made articles command. Two firms, one German and one American, do business in the capital; but the bulk of their trade is with the palace and the government directly, in the furnishing of arms, Gatling guns, and furniture, and, of course, the inevitable champagne and liquor. These commodities are fortunately too high-priced for the masses, so there is less danger than might be expected of the corruption of the Corean people by the introduction of fiery drinks. The most important imports from England are unbleached muslin, out of which clothing is made, rice and silk from Japan, and silk from China. A curious penchant of Coreans is for cuckoo clocks. The cuckoo is a native of the peninsula, and people seem never tired of entering a store and listening to the cry of the birds which come out of the clocks and tell the hour. Dozens of these are kept in the Chinese stores, and they sell readily at a good profit.

It must be remembered that the average commercial transaction is very small. The coin of Corea is the "cash," which, however, is not uniform over the country. The piece in use at the capital, which is called a five-cash piece, has about the value of an eighth of a penny. Five pounds' worth of this coinage is a load for a coolie. The comparative smallness of even the largest Corean transaction can be seen from this. In dealings with foreign countries the Mexican dollar used to be the basis, but as it was greatly debased and sweated and tampered with by the Chinese, it has been largely replaced by the Japanese *yen*, a beautiful coin engraved with such fine designs and so excellently milled that even the Chinese experts at stealing silver from coins and plugging them up are unable to operate upon it.

With patience, and with the development of resources, a respectable trade will doubtless be established with the once hermit nation; yet the country cannot be in a fair way to a prosperous condition, until it learns to develop what must prove to be its main sources of reliance—a better system of agriculture, and the opening of mining industries by foreign capital (until Coreans have learned how such operations should be carried on), in all this acting with more candour and less distrust toward the people to whom it must commit the developing of its resources. With the customs left under its present able and honest management, a very few years would see Corea rivalling Japan in the advance toward wealth and prosperity.

CHAPTER XII.

PROGRESS.

COREA has now been a member of the family of nations for eight years, and naturally the thoughtful are beginning to ask what has been accomplished. Japan on the one side has made wonderful strides. Her people are doing all they can to become Westernized. A constitution similar to that of some of the European governments has been adopted. The government, from being an absolute monarchy, has now become a constitutional government, with its provisions copied from, or suggested by, European instruments. In fact, Japan is losing a great deal of its Orientalism. Such is the tendency of one of Corea's great neighbours. Now, what of the other? As Japan represents the radical or progressive, China represents the ultra-conservative. Hardly a step toward Occidentalism does she take without being forced. Those, therefore, who know the tendencies of these nations have naturally been watching carefully to see which of them Corea will follow—Japan and Occidentalism, or China and the Oriental conservatism.

Let us see what has been done. First, as to educational steps. A royal school was established in 1886, and has been most successful. If the excellent system thus begun in the capital is extended throughout the country, the development of the peninsula will be not a probability but a certainty. In Seoul there are also several mission schools which are well attended.

In the direction of the development of the military power much has been attempted. The native firearms of Corea are of course very ineffective, as compared with modern Western weapons. Accordingly several battalions have been armed with modern breech-loaders, and, I believe, some with magazine rifles. (Not the least curious of the sights to be seen on the king's parades is the appearance of companies marching side by side, one carrying the old flint-locks, or match-locks fired with punk, and the other armed with breech-loaders and sabre bayonets.) In line with this new equipment was the purchase of several Gatling guns, and practice with these is frequent, especially as the noise is pleasing to His Majesty. The uniform of most of the soldiers has been changed from its picturesque, though somewhat inconvenient form, and is supposed now to be modelled after the Western military style; but as the material is dyed cotton, and the dye fades with all degrees of irregularity, and since the cut of the clothing is decidedly *sui generis*, the aspect of the companies on march is peculiar rather than picturesque.

AN ABORTIVE REFORM.

It will be seen, then, that there has been an attempt to model the army after a European pattern, but one cannot say that it has been successful.

In 1888 four officers, three from the United States and one from Japan, were called in to train a corps of cadets, and so to extend instruction to the four thousand troops or so in the capital. But after these men had come, and attempted to begin work, they found themselves hampered and harassed so that they could accomplish nothing. Add to this the fact that their salaries were for months not forthcoming, and it will be seen that this venture was one of disaster for all concerned. Hardly any instruction has been given, money has been expended in a change of uniforms, and but little real benefit has resulted from the engagement of these gentlemen. There might be added to these miscarriages the expenditure in erecting a powder-mill which makes no powder.

Now, Corea is in a peculiar position. She is sandwiched in between Japan and China, two very strong nations. She therefore needs either a very strong army, so as to present at least a show of resistance in case of attack, or else an army simply for police duty. But the very largest army Corea can raise could not carry on a successful war. Were she to arm all her available fighting force, to call out every male capable of bearing arms, she could not oppose with any success the forces of either Japan or China. At present her men are undrilled, her resources are undeveloped, she has no weapons, and there is no military obstacle in the way of a regiment of experienced soldiers marching the length of the land, carrying everything before them. No movement has been made for fortifying the keys of the capital, or for replacing the native cannon with modern guns. The government is as yet too poor.

In a third way Corea has started on Western paths. In her treaties, the right to admit and to send diplomatic officers is given. She has also in various countries merchants who act as her consuls, though as yet there is no business demanding their attention.

Other advances and attempts have been made, the fruits of which have not as yet been realized. In 1884, under the administration of a radical government, preparations had been made to enter the postal union. The stamps had been printed, and all arrangements completed; a banquet was held at the Foreign Office to rejoice over and celebrate the consummation of this work. While the banquet was in progress, Min Yong Ik, the confidential agent of the king, staggered into the banqueting-hall, covered with blood flowing from numerous wounds. An attempt had been made by the radicals to assassinate him, because he was supposed to have drawn back from the policy of advance. An *emeute* followed. The radicals fled because of the revulsion of feeling caused by their action. The feeling of hatred to the foreigners was fanned by the conservative or Chinese party. For a

A NATIONAL MINT.   115

few days there was danger of a rising which would sweep away every foreigner in the country. But gradually the excitement died out; people saw that the trouble was not due to the foreigners, but to hasty and ill-balanced officials, who could not make progress slowly, and the resentment against outsiders little by little faded away. But the post-office was defunct. The Corean postage stamps are sought by collectors because they are a curiosity, having never been used. Though mails are distributed in Corea, it is by the Japanese government, which maintains offices, collects all the revenue, and does all the work arising from this source.

Another direction in which it was hoped progress would be made, and in which steps have been taken, is in the establishment of a national mint. The best machinery was bought and placed in position, designs were made and dies cut, and in 1888 the mint was completed, the wheels revolved a few times, a couple of hundred copper coins were turned out for the inspection of the king, who paid a visit to the new toy, and then the wheels were stopped. Since then the machinery has stood idle and rusting, the German expert who erected it has returned to his home, and the work of nearly two years, at an expense of perhaps forty thousand pounds, remains as so much outlay without any corresponding return.

We have had occasion to speak of the custom of signalling daily along the tops of the hills the news of the peace and welfare of the kingdom. Alongside of this medieval system of despatching news must be placed the modern way of using the electric current, since for years the capital has been connected by wire with the southern port of Fusan, with its own port of Chemulpo, and with the capital of China, and so with the whole outside world. Corea, the hermit nation of 1882, in telegraphic communication with the isles of the West in 1885!

In the domestic life of the nation but little change has been caused by the opening of treaty relations with other nations. But few Coreans have changed their manner of living.

The revenue from imports is increasing largely each year, proving that Western products are taking their place in the domestic economy of the people. And with each importation and its use among the people, a wider interest in the nation from which the article comes is excited, and so progress is made.

CHAPTER XIII.

FOREIGN RELATIONS.

THE geographical position of Corea exposes that small kingdom to the attentions, not always disinterested, of her powerful neighbours—China, Japan, and Russia. She is most naturally connected with China, of which the Corean peninsula is an extension. China's suzerainty over Corea is generally admitted, although the securities on which it rests are very vague. No one can be surprised at the desire of China to convert that indefinite superiority into a closer bond by the annexation of the peninsula. Not less intelligible, however, is the objection of Japan to an extension of Chinese territory which would bring its powerful rival within an hundred miles of its western coast. It has no doubt been with a view of preventing this contingency that Japan has been striving for some years to increase her influence in Corea, and to detach that kingdom from China. Corea's third neighbour is Russia, whose Maritime Province of Siberia is conterminous for a few miles with the Corean frontier. Russia has shown no inclination to interfere in the recent controversies of China and Japan over this new Eastern Question; she has even taken the trouble to deny that she had intervened. Obviously, however, Russia has a very direct interest in the matter in dispute, and it need not be doubted that Russian diplomacy will be ready to take its share in the work whenever that may be necessary. Russian statesmen have always shown a remarkable capacity for biding their time. The same reasons which made it important that Russia should obtain the coast of Manchuria south of the Amoor a few years ago, would make it important that she should include Corea in her Maritime Province. In any case she would certainly do her utmost to prevent the peninsula from falling into the hands of any other state.

In the meantime China and Japan are the only claimants for influence in Corea. The question is an important one for Japan; but to China it is more than important—it is vital. If Japan were to secure a foothold on the continent, such as the possession of Corea would give her, she would be forced by the circumstances of the case to extend her encroachments if possible into the heart of the Chinese Empire. Recent events seem to show that a struggle of that kind may be imminent. Japan is evidently eager for the fray, and China, though her government has shown no desire to precipitate matters, is evidently ready to take up the gauntlet, and is prepared, in the words of her ablest

FOREIGN RELATIONS. 119

statesman, "to fight to the bitter end." The conflict will be an interesting one for the student of history. It will be a struggle in the far east of Asia between the new civilization and the old—between Western ideas and methods of administration and diplomacy and the most stagnant of Oriental despotisms.

Only in quite recent times has Corea been induced to enter into diplomatic relations with foreign states. The earliest efforts in that direction were made by France and by the United States of America in 1871, and they failed. The first treaty that the King of Corea is known to have signed was concluded in 1876, and that was a treaty with Japan. The immediate practical purpose of the Japanese government was to obtain protection and trading privileges for Japanese residents in Corea, who numbered several thousands. Under this treaty also the Japanese government was entitled to send a permanent resident to the capital of Corea; three ports were opened to Japanese trade —namely, Chemulpo, Fusan, and Gen-san; Japanese vessels in distress were allowed to enter Corean ports; and Japanese mariners were free to survey the Corean coast. Probably, however, the treaty was intended also to serve a diplomatic purpose—that, namely, of putting the King of Corea in the position of an independent sovereign, having power to make treaties with other states. It is difficult to understand how the king reconciled his action with his acknowledged subjection to the suzerainty of China. That consideration did not trouble the Japanese government. That government has never denied the suzerainty of China over Corea, but it has advanced the opinion that that relation was not inconsistent with the right of the King of Corea to make treaties with other states. Japan maintained the same position in 1885, when a new treaty was made; and again in 1894, when the Corean question led to war.

The second recorded treaty into which Corea entered was made with China in 1882. The fact that China entered into such a relation has been held to be a recognition by China of the independence of Corea. It is not usual for a government to make treaties with a subject state. A treaty is a mutual agreement implying the equality of the high contracting parties. China, however, maintains that the so-called treaty of 1882 was not a treaty in the strict sense—was, in fact, no more than a body of "commercial and trade regulations for the subjects of China and Corea." Clearly there was nothing improper or unusual in a suzerain state issuing such regulations, or in a subject state accepting them.

In the same year (1882) Corea made a treaty with the United States; and that was followed, during the next four or five years, by treaties with Germany, Great Britain, Italy, Russia, and France. All these countries seem to have dealt with the Corean king as an independent and autonomous sovereign.

Japan succeeded in concluding a second treaty with

INTERNAL REFORMS. 121

Corea in 1885, which greatly strengthened her hold on the peninsula and its government. That treaty is of the greatest importance, because it forms the foundation of the subsequent action of Japan in Corean affairs. It established the right of Japan equally with China to send troops to Corea in case of disturbance or other emergency. If China did not sanction this treaty, she certainly did not make objection to it. Indeed, at the time, her diplomatic hands were fully occupied with an embroilment with France, and probably Japan took advantage of China's difficulties in order to extort the treaty from the King of Corea.

Japan has missed no opportunity of taking advantage of the improved position which the treaty of 1885 gave her. She has pressed on the Corean government the necessity of internal reforms; she has sought to obtain privileges for the Japanese residents in Corea; and she has declared her desire to be the champion of the independence of that kingdom.

The question of internal reforms was taken up eagerly by a strong party in Corea, consisting in the first instance chiefly of Japanese, and they had an able Japanese leader. The outbreak of what is known as the Tokugato rebellion in 1893 gave the Japanese government an opportunity of acting on the treaty of 1885. Such a disturbance had occurred as seemed to warrant armed intervention. The hostile feeling was imbittered by an incident. The rebel leader, when driven out of Corea, took refuge in Japan. After he had resided there for some months, he was enticed to Shanghai, and was there murdered by order of the King of Corea, with the complicity, it is alleged, of the Chinese authorities.

When the King of Corea applied to China for military aid to put down the Tokugato rebellion, the Chinese government resolved to send a force of 10,000 men. As soon as Japan heard of this intention, the Mikado despatched a force of 5,000 men of all arms, well equipped and organized, which succeeded in reaching Corea before the Chinese troops.

In taking this step the Japanese disclaimed hostile intentions. Their professed objects were to protect their countrymen, and "to co-operate with the Chinese" in restoring order. At the same time, they renewed their claim to deal with the King of Corea as an independent ruler. They maintained that they had the same rights in Corea as China had, excepting always the Chinese suzerainty, which was not to be interfered with, "but was to retain its historical and ceremonial character."

The Japanese government also submitted to the king twenty-five proposals for internal reforms. In the first instance the king agreed to accept these proposals, but afterwards he made his acceptance of them conditional on the withdrawal of the Japanese troops. China, as was to be expected, supported the

WAR DECLARED. 123

king in refusing reform, and further demanded the withdrawal of the Japanese army.

In the midst of the diplomatic controversy hostilities suddenly broke out. On July 25, 1894, a Japanese squadron attacked a Chinese fleet that was convoying to Corea a transport vessel, the *Kow Shing*, with fifteen hundred men on board. The transport was sunk, and only a few of the men were saved. As war had not been declared, it rested with the Japanese government to explain this wanton violation of peace. The explanation offered was that the Japanese commander was under the impression that China "intended to begin hostilities." It turned out that the *Kow Shing* was a British vessel chartered by the Chinese government, and flying the British flag. The Japanese government found it necessary to apologise to the British representative at Tokio, and to promise compensation. There were other collisions between the forces of the two countries, both at sea and on land. In this state of matters the Japanese government, on July 31, intimated to the foreign representatives at Tokio that "a state of war existed between China and Japan," Corea being the bone of contention between them.

The following figures regarding the fighting strength of the two countries may be interesting:—

CHINESE ARMY.

On peace footing.....................................	200,000 men.
On war footing.......................................	600,000 men.
Capable of being raised to.........................	1,200,000 men.

CHINESE NAVY.

Battleships—1 first-class, 1 second-class, 3 third-class. Port defence vessels, 9. Cruisers—9 second-class, 12 third-class (*a*), and 35 third-class (*b*). Torpedo boats—2 first-class, 26 second-class, 13 third-class, and 2 smaller boats.

JAPANESE ARMY.

On peace footing .... **78,000** men.
On war footing .... **250,000** men.

JAPANESE NAVY.

Armoured cruisers, **5**; second-class cruisers, **9**; third-class cruisers, **22**.

₊ The above figures are taken from the *Statesman's Year Book* for 1894.

CHAPTER XIV.

MISSIONS.

THIS little book should not be closed without a word about the missions to Corea.

Roman Catholic priests pushed their way into the country from China as early as the end of last century, and the missions they established were very successful, their converts numbering many thousands. Several times during the present century the Corean Catholics have been subjected to bitter persecution notably in 1868, when thousands of them were killed, and the only three Catholic missionaries left had to flee for their lives. In spite of persecutions there are still many Catholics in Corea.

The beginning of Protestant evangelization is due to Rev. John Ross, a missionary in China, who visited the country and translated the New Testament into Corean.

The actual occupation of the country as a mission field did not begin till 1884, when Dr. Allen was sent out to the capital by the Presbyterian Church of the United States.

Dr. Allen was not known at first as a missionary. He went ostensibly to practise his profession as a physician. The unfortunate postal *emeute* of 1884, and the attack upon Min Yong Ik, next to the king the most prominent person in the kingdom, by giving Dr. Allen an opportunity of displaying upon the young prince the skill of Western medical science, opened the way for more direct mission work. His success in bringing Min Yong Ik through his illness led to his being asked to prescribe for the king and other members of the royal family. Success attended him here. He was consulted in other matters, and his conservatism and the common sense of his advice gained for him the entire confidence of the king.

In a conversation with the king, some time after the *emeute*, the work of the hospitals in Western lands was brought to his attention, and the description the doctor gave of their operation and benefits interested the king so much that he suggested, or acted upon the suggestion of Dr. Allen, that one be established in the capital. This was warmly welcomed by Dr. Allen, and buildings were set apart for the purpose, a certain sum was devoted to its maintenance, and Dr. Allen became the head of it, while mandarins were detailed to look after its management, and servants were appointed for doing the necessary work.

In the following year more missionaries were sent out by the United States Presbyterians, and in a short time they succeeded in organizing a school of medicine connected with the hospital, and an orphanage, both of which have been most successful.

Missionaries have also been sent to Corea by the Methodists of the United States, the Presbyterians of Canada and Australia, and lastly the Church of England. Their work has been hitherto centred in the capital; but the English bishop has taken a forward step in establishing a station in the south of Corea.

What is the position of missionaries in Corea at the present time? There is no open government sanction for the active work of evangelization; indeed, the treaties made with foreign nations do not permit it. As a matter of fact, however, the government has winked at the prosecution of the missionaries' labours. No open preaching is permitted, and even teaching is prohibited; but evangelistic work is done by the circulation of literature and by conversation with those who go to the missionaries for instruction.

As for the converts to Christianity, their position is not perfectly safe. The machinery which wrought destruction among the Roman Catholics is still in existence; the only question is as to the disposition to put it into operation against the Christians. From what has been said already, it has been seen that the government does not interfere with missionary work, beyond warning missionaries now and again not to push forward their cause too openly. During the last few years trouble has several times appeared imminent, and on one occasion a massacre might easily have been precipitated, but no unseemly act was committed, and no Protestant convert, so far as is known, has suffered for renouncing the faith of his fathers.

THE END.

www.ingramcontent.com/pod-product-compliance
Lightning Source LLC
Chambersburg PA
CBHW031600170426
43196CB00032B/743